MONASTIC WISDOM SEI

Robert Thomas, ocso

Passing from Self to God
A Cistercian Retreat

MONASTIC WISDOM SERIES

Patrick Hart, ocso, General Editor

Advisory Board

Michael Casey, ocso   Terrence Kardong, osb
Lawrence S. Cunningham   Kathleen Norris
Bonnie Thurston   Miriam Pollard, ocso

MONASTIC WISDOM SERIES: NUMBER SIX

Passing from Self to God

A Cistercian Retreat

Robert Thomas, ocso

Translated by
Martha F. Krieg

CISTERCIAN PUBLICATIONS
Kalamazoo, Michigan

Originally published as:
Passer de soi-même à Dieu
(Saint-Foy, Québec: Éditions Anne Sigler, 1990)

Cistercian Publications
Editorial Offices
The Institute of Cistercian Studies
Western Michigan University
Kalamazoo, Michigan 49008-5415
cistpub@wmich.edu

The work of Cistercian Publications is made possible in part by support from Western Michigan University to The Institute of Cistercian Studies.

Library of Congress Cataloging-in-Publication Data

Thomas, Robert, moine de Sept-Fons.
 [Passer de soi-même à Dieu. English]
 Passing from self to God : a Cistercian retreat / Robert Thomas ; translated by Martha F. Krieg.
  p. cm. — (Monastic wisdom series ; no. 6)
 Includes bibliographical references (p.   ) and indexes.
 ISBN-13: 978-0-87907-006-9 (alk. paper)
 ISBN-10: 0-87907-006-4 (alk. paper)
 1. Cistercians—Spiritual life. 2. Spiritual retreats for members of religious orders. I. Title. II. Series.

BX3403.T46 2006
269'.694—dc22   2006004869

TABLE OF CONTENTS

TRANSLATOR'S INTRODUCTION

Fr Robert Thomas was a venerable Cistercian monk, living in the abbey of Sept-Fons in France. Several decades ago, he became concerned that the written heritage of the Cistercian Fathers was increasingly inaccessible to the new generation of French monks, because the works existed primarily in Latin. So he began a series of translations, Pain de Cîteaux (Bread of Cîteaux). This series has been very helpful in expanding the availability of the thought of the Cistercians to French-speakers, in the same way that the Cistercian Publications series have been useful to English-speakers.

In 1995, I had the privilege of encountering Fr Thomas at the Cistercian Studies meetings in Kalamazoo, at which he was honored for his role in the preservation of Cistercian life. I was struck by his radiant serenity and sense of humor. Another presenter was a nun of a certain age who had made a retreat of some months' duration under his direction. Fr Thomas had set her to copying out by hand, in Latin, some of the Cistercian works. My immediate reaction was a strong desire to have a retreat under his direction. However, several children still at home and a full-time job made that unlikely. Browsing the Cistercian Publications bookstall later that day, I found his book, *Passer de soi-même à Dieu: Une retraite cistercienne (Passing from Self to God: A Cistercian Retreat)*. After reading it, it seemed to me that it might be interesting to other English-speakers as well, and Dr Elder agreed.

This book is an accessible introduction to monastic wisdom. It will be useful to those who seek the path to God, as individuals or as a group, as laypeople or as religious. Because it quotes extensively from the writings of the Cistercian Fathers, including

Saint Bernard, William of Saint-Thierry, Aelred of Rievaulx, and many others, it is also a palatable introduction to the writings of the Fathers. It is not necessary to decide which one of the many works to begin with, nor is it necessary to brace oneself for the onslaught of an entire tractate or book written in medieval rhetorical style, in order to discover what attracted these men to desire God so strongly. The best news is that what they sought and found is still available to each of us today.

The cited works have been taken from Cistercian Publications editions when possible. For the non-scholars among you, it may at first be disorienting to find that the footnotes give the author's name and a cryptic abbreviation based on the Latin name of the work. There is a table of the abbreviations, and soon you will find them no more difficult than "LotR" or "RotK" (referring to J. R. R. Tolkien's *Lord of the Rings* trilogy, and the third book in it, *The Return of the King*). The numbers following the abbreviation refer to the sermon/tractate/chapter, then the section. The Cistercian Fathers series reference is in the form CF 3:167, referring to volume 3, page 167. So a complete reference to a sentence in the first section of William of Saint-Thierry's *Twelfth Meditation* would read: William, Med 12.1; CF 3:167.

I would like to thank Dr Rozanne Elder for her encouragement and patience. Ms Jean Curtiss was of great assistance in reading the first draft. The whole project would not have been possible without the support of my husband Laurence and my children, Katy, Elissa, and Ian, and our Japanese daughter Megumi. And thank you, Fr Thomas, because in the end, after translating, looking up the correct Cistercian Publications texts for the quotations where such existed, and revising, I find that I have spent months under your tutelage after all.

Martha F. Krieg

26 February 2005, Ypsilanti, Michigan

PREFACE

Here we are on a retreat. It will revolve around this idea:
Passing from self to God. That is simple Christian spirituality,
which is rooted in Jesus' passage from death to life; it is a
spirituality of passage, a paschal spirituality.

But what makes this a *Cistercian* retreat? A huge number of
ideas and texts have been borrowed from the great Cistercian
spiritual masters of the twelfth century.

People more or less know Saint Bernard; a few people also
know a little bit about William of Saint-Thierry. They are not the
only authors from the first years of Cîteaux. There are also the
Blessed Guerric of Igny, Saint Aelred of Rievaulx, Isaac of Stella,
Gilbert of Hoyland, and still more, with whom you are going
to become acquainted and who will, I firmly hope, help you to
recollect yourself, to pray.

Allow me to refer often to "our Fathers" when speaking
of these authors. They are Cistercians, but above all Christians,
men of the Church, and so they belong to all of us. They are ours,
they are yours.

Brief introduction to the authors

Bernard of Clairvaux (1090–1153)

Having entered Cîteaux at the age of twenty-one, he was
sent to found Clairvaux three years later. Sought more and more
from all sides, he engaged in an unusual number of activities. On
his numerous trips, in the midst of crowds, he made solitude for
himself in his heart; he remained a monk. He performed countless
miracles, but remained humble.

William of Saint-Thierry (about 1075–1148)

At first a Benedictine, and even an important abbot of that order, he entered the young Cistercian foundation of Signy, in the Ardennes, in 1135. A remarkable spiritual and mystical theologian, he was also a great friend of Saint Bernard.

Guerric of Igny (about 1075–1157)

A canon of Tournay, he went to visit Clairvaux and stayed there. He was formed by Saint Bernard for some fifteen years, and has a theology of the formation of Christ within us. The Virgin Mary watches over that formation. His works (fifty-four sermons) are well written.

Aelred of Rievaulx (1110–1166)

After a rather turbulent youth, he entered Rievaulx, an English foundation of Clairvaux, at the age of twenty-four. He was a man of great sweetness. The first of his very numerous works was the *Mirror of Charity*, written at the order of Saint Bernard (his father-immediate, the abbot of the founding house).

Isaac of Stella (?–about 1178)

Very well educated, a powerful spirit, above all a great mystic, he probably entered monastic life at Pontigny (Yonne). He became abbot of "L'Étoile" (Star Abbey), in the diocese of Poitiers, then of Nôtre Dame des Châteliers, on the isle of Ré.

Gilbert of Hoyland (?–1172)

English like the two preceding writers, he worked on, but did not finish, the commentary on the *Song of Songs* begun by Saint Bernard. He too was a great mystic, and very insightful. He loved to speak of love and of prayer.

Baldwin of Ford (?–1190)

He was also an Englishman. Archdeacon of Totnes, he entered the abbey of Ford, of which he became abbot in 1175. Promoted to the bishopric of Worcester in 1180, he became archbishop of Canterbury. He accompanied his king, Richard the Lion-Hearted, on Crusade and died under the walls of Tyre. He wrote a treatise on the *Sacrament of the Altar* and several others, in which the theme of the love of God frequently recurs.

John of Ford (1140–1214)

He confessed to having lived the life of a sinner in the world. Once at Ford, he became Baldwin's secretary, and later his prior. He finished the commentary on the *Song of Songs* in one hundred twenty sermons.

Helinand of Froidmont (?–1230)

A troubadour who entered Froidmont, he wrote some sermons, a universal chronicle, and three treatises. He had a great devotion to the Blessed Virgin.

Adam of Perseigne (about 1145–about 1221)

A canon regular, and later a Benedictine before becoming a Cistercian, he speaks often of the Virgin Mary in his sermons and letters.

This list only contains the authors cited during the course of this retreat.

LIST OF ABBREVIATIONS

Series

CC   Corpus Christianorum series, Turnhout, Belgium. 1953–

CF   Cistercian Fathers series. Spencer, Massachusetts, Kalamazoo, Michigan, 1970–

PC   *Pain de Cîteaux* series. Chambarand, France; Chimay, Belgium; Dompierre-sur-Besbre, France; Oka, Québec, 1959–

PL   J.-P. Migne, *Patrologiae cursus completus, series latina,* 221 volumes. Paris, 1844–1864.

SCh   Sources chrétiennes series. Paris: Cerf, 1941–

Authors and Works

Adam of Perseigne
Epp   *Epistolae*—Letters

Aelred of Rievaulx
Adv   *Sermo in adventu domini*—Sermon on the Advent of the Lord

Am spir *De spirituali amicitia*—On Spiritual Friendship

Inst incl *De institutione inclusarum*—Rule of Life for a Recluse

Oner   *Sermo de oneribus*—Sermon on burdens

PP   *Sermo in solemnitate Petri et Pauli de tribus portis et tribus templis*—Sermon on the Solemnity of Peter and Paul of the three doors and the three temples

SI   *Sermones ineditos*—Unedited sermons

Spec car   *Speculum caritatis*—Mirror of Charity

Baldwin of Ford

Sac altar   *De sacramento altaris*—Sacrament of the Altar

Tract   *Tractati*—Tractates

Vita coen   *De vita coenobitica*—On the Cenobitic or Common Life

Bernard of Clairvaux

Adv   *Sermo in adventu domini*—Sermon for the Advent of the Lord

Asc   *Sermo in ascensione domini*—Sermon for the Ascension of the Lord

Cin   *Sermo in feria quarta cinerum*—Sermon for Ash Wednesday

Conv   *Sermo de conversione ad clericos*—Sermon on conversion to the clergy

Conv P   *Sermo de conversione sancti Pauli*—Sermon for the Conversion of St Paul

Dil   *Liber de diligendo Deo*—On Loving God

Div   *Sermones de diversis*—Sermons on various subjects

Epi   *Sermo in epiphania domini*—Sermon for the Epiphany of the Lord

Epp   *Epistolae*—Letters

Hum   *Liber de gradibus humilitatis et superbiae*—The Steps of Humility & Pride

SC   *Sermo super* Cantica canticorum—Sermon on the Song of Songs

Gilbert of Hoyland

SC   *Sermo super* Cantica canticorum—Sermon on the Song of Songs

Tract   *Tractati*—Tractates

Guerric of Igny

SC   *Sermo super* Cantica canticorum—Sermon on the
          Song of Songs

Helinand

Palm   *Sermo in ramis palmarum*—Sermon for Palm Sunday

Isaac of Stella

Asspt   *Sermo in assumptione BVM*—Sermon for the
          Assumption of the Blessed Virgin Mary

JB   *Sermo in nativitate sancti Ioannis Baptistae*—Sermon
          for the Birth of John the Baptist

OS   *Sermo in festivitate Omnium Sanctorum*—Sermon
          for All Saints' Day

Quad   *Sermo in quadragesima*—Sermon for Lent

John of Ford

SC   *Sermo super* Cantica canticorum—Sermon on the
          Song of Songs

William of Saint-Thierry

Ænig   *Ænigma fidei*—The Enigma of Faith

Cant   *Expositio super* Cantica canticorum—Exposition on
          the Song of Songs

Contemp   *De contemplando Deo*—On Contemplating God

Ep frat   *Epistola [aurea] ad fratres de Monte Dei*—The Golden
          Epistle

Exp Rm   *Expositio in epistolam Pauli ad Romanos*—Exposition
          on the Epistle of Paul to the Romans

Nat am   *De natura et dignitate amoris*—On the Nature and
          Dignity of Love

Nat corp *De natura corporis et animae*—On the Nature of the
          Body and the Soul

Med   *Meditativae orationes*—Meditations

Sac altar *De sacramento altaris liber*—On the Sacrament of the
          Altar

Spec fid   *Speculum fidei*—Mirror of Faith

Vita Bern   *Sancti Bernardi vita prima*—The First Biography of
St Bernard, translation cited as *Vita Prima*

Scriptural Citations

Genesis	Gn	Daniel	Dn
Exodus	Ex	Hosea	Hos
Leviticus	Lv	Joel	Jl
Numbers	Nm	Amos	Am
Deuteronomy	Dt	Obadiah	Ob
Joshua	Jos	Jonah	Jon
Judges	Jgs	Micah	Mi
Ruth	Ru	Nahum	Na
1 Samuel	1 Sm	Zephaniah	Zep
2 Samuel	2 Sm	Haggai	Hg
1 Chronicles	1 Chr	Zechariah	Zec
2 Chronicles	2 Chr	Malachi	Mal
Ezra	Ezr	Matthew	Mat
Nehemiah	Neh	Mark	Mk
Tobit	Tb	Luke	Lk
Judith	Jdt	John	Jn
Esther	Est	Acts	Acts
1 Maccabees	1 Mc	Romans	Rom
2 Maccabees	2 Mc	1 Corinthians	1 Cor
Job	Jb	2 Corinthians	2 Cor
Psalms	Ps(s)	Galatians	Gal
Proverbs	Prv	Ephesians	Eph
Ecclesiastes	Qo	Philippians	Phil
Song of Songs	Sg	Colossians	Col
Wisdom	Ws	1 Thessalonians	1 Thes
Sirach	Si	2 Thessalonians	2 Thes
Ecclesiasticus		1 Timothy	1 Tm
Isaiah	Is	2 Timothy	2 Tm
Jeremiah	Jer	Titus	Ti
Lamentations	Lam	Philemon	Phlm
Baruch	Bar	Hebrews	Heb
Ezekiel	Ez	James	Jas

1 Peter	1 Pt	Jude	Jude
2 Peter	2 Pt	Revelation	Rv
1 John	1 Jn		
2 John	2 Jn	Revised Standard	
3 John	3 Jn	Version	RSV

I ATMOSPHERE OF THE RETREAT

The theme of this retreat is, as we said, going from oneself to God. Our spiritual authors, our Cistercian Fathers, considered themselves Hebrews, that is to say, "people of passage" (wanderers) (*transeuntes, transilientes*): as people who had passed from the world to the monastery, from the temporal to the eternal, finally from self to God, as William of Saint Thierry phrases it. When we see different references to rest in God, struggle against the old man, spiritual infancy, forgetfulness of self, praise of God, the will of God to be done more than our own, finally faith in the love of God, it always amounts in the end to this same theme of passing from self to God.

There is a great unity in Cistercian spirituality, and that spirituality can still be summed up by the phrase which formerly had the same sense of passage from self to God: passing from multiplicity to unity. If you have read *The Monastic Day*,[1] you will have noticed this unity. Through all the bodily and spiritual exercises (to borrow an expression from William), there is always the same deepening tendency, the soul of the Benedictine and Cistercian life: to live in the presence of God, in relation with him, to pray, to love without ceasing.

In this first address, I am going to give you a few evocative words, which will put us into the retreat atmosphere.

Intus

Intus, within. Monastic life, but also a retreat, is a life or a time when we are drawn out of the world, when we learn to

1. Robert Thomas, *La journée monastique*. Pain de Cîteaux series. (Paris: O.E.I.L., 1985).

1

live within, to enter into ourselves, to return to our heart. In his *Thirty-first Sermon on Various Subjects*, Saint Bernard borrows this word from Scripture,[2] and treats it as a synonym for monk;[3] in his *Ninth Sermon*, he exhorts his monks to walk in the ways of their hearts, to hold their souls in their hands unceasingly:

> to hear what the Lord God says in you, because he speaks of peace. But who are those people to whom he speaks so? *Surely those who come back to their hearts.*[4]

Bernard made postulants who presented themselves in haste to enter, put the brakes on, to show them what direction they should take in their haste, the real direction of their monastic life:

> If you are in such a hurry for what is inside
> *si ad ea quæ **intus** sunt festinatis.*[5]

Notice these two themes of *haste* and of *interiority*: a monk and anyone who is intent on living with God, under God's gaze, is in a hurry, on fire, dynamic, and someone who tends toward recollection, toward the interior life, *someone who hastens toward interior things*.

This word *intus* is found quite often in our Fathers to characterize our life: in Bernard, William, Gilbert, Baldwin, and John of Ford, Adam of Perseigne; I could easily cite a few texts.

To descend in one's interior, to live with oneself

We are seeking God. If we seek him with sincerity, perseverance and frequency, we are sure, says Saint Bernard, to find him:

> It is more likely that earth and heaven will pass away than that such a seeker will not find him.[6]

2. Ps 86.
3. Bernard, Div 31.1.
4. Bernard, Div 9.2.
5. William, Vita Bern, I.20; *Vita Prima*, 27.
6. Bernard, Div 37.9.

This is reassuring. But where do we seek God in order to find him? Once more Saint Bernard answers and again reassures us: it is not necessary to search for him far way, there is no need to cross the Alps or the seas:

> You have only to descend into yourself to find him. *Usque ad temetipsum occurre Deo tuo.*[7]

This is what Saint Benedict did who, as Saint Gregory the Great says, *lived with himself* under the gaze of the divine Onlooker when he lived in a cave for three years; as he also surely did throughout his life.

The teaching of the Cistercian spiritual writers, speaking both of their theology and of their spiritual life, is strongly rooted in the *theme of the image.* A phrase from his *Sermons on the Song* tells us how, for Bernard, this doctrine of the soul created in the image of God is bound up with that of the return of the person within himself.

> For "God is a spirit,"[8] and those who wish to persevere in or attain to his likeness *must enter into their hearts,* and apply themselves spiritually to that work, until "with unveiled face, beholding the glory of the Lord," *they "become transfigured into the same likeness,* borrowing glory from that glory, as the Spirit of the Lord enables them."[9]

Baldwin also speaks of this dwelling with God that benefits the person who lives with himself, when he is recollected:

> The just man dwells in the tabernacle of his heart where God also dwells.[10]

When two people live together in a house, it is easy to meet one another: to live *with, in* one's self in order to find God there.

Isaac has this beautiful thought which can provide a complete program for the interior life, a life of intimacy with God:

---

7. Bernard, Adv 1.10.
8. Jn 4:24.
9. 2 Cor 3:18. Bernard, SC 24.5; CF 7:46. Emphasis added.
10. Baldwin, Tract 5; CF 39:139.

> So, brother, make for yourself a hidden place within yourself,
> in which you can flee away from yourself and pray in secret
> to the Father.[11]

We should take note of these two attitudes toward *the self*: you must flee yourself and nevertheless come back into yourself. You must forget yourself and nevertheless be concerned with yourself, know yourself. It is necessary to hate yourself and nevertheless to love yourself.

Isn't this same idea found in these lines by the blessed Elisabeth of the Trinity:

> As to Zaccheus, my Master said to me: "Hurry and come
> down, I must stay at your place." Hurry to come down,
> but where? To the very depths of myself; after having left
> myself, separated myself from myself, stripped myself of
> myself, in a word: without myself.[12]

Intus, within. This is one word. *A hiding place*, to live within that hiding place, there's a second word. Let us add a third: to enclose yourself.

Enclosing yourself

To put ourselves in the atmosphere of the retreat, we could also meditate on these words which **William** addresses to the Carthusians of Mont-Dieu:

> You have shut out the world, whole and entire, from yourselves
> and shut up yourselves, whole and entire, with God.[13]

This calls to mind another of the phrases that he uses in one of his meditations, when he begins to pray and says to God:

> All other things excluded, I can shut myself away with you,
> O Truth, alone.[14]

11. Isaac, OS 1; PL 194, 1691D; CF 11:5.
12. Last Retreat, 16th day.
13. William, Ep frat I.10; CF 12:20.
14. William, Med 9; CF 3:147. In the original French translations of the Latin, Fr Thomas used *exclu*, "excluded," and *inclus*, "included," with a note that the translation was very literal on purpose.

This is what a retreat is, above all in the strong times of prayer: we exclude everything else, there is nothing left but God.

We descend to the bottom of our hearts and there we find God. Charles de Foucauld wrote to his sister, a married woman:

> God is in us, at the bottom of our soul,
> always, always listening to us there,
> and asking us to chat a little with him.
> From time to time lower your eyes towards your chest,
> recollect yourself a quarter of a minute, and say:
> "You are there, my God, I love you."

We recollect ourselves, go down into ourselves, and **William** says, *we find what to be occupied with*:

Occupied with self, occupied with God

It is the double goal of the monk in the cloister, says **Saint Bernard**; but who will stop us from saying: the double goal of any true believer in Jesus Christ, because, we must not forget, it was to all his disciples that Jesus said: "Pray always, and never cease,"[15] and again: "Be perfect as your heavenly Father is perfect;"[16] double goal of the person who isolates himself from everything, as much as is possible for him, in order to recollect himself and meet God. Referring to a famous phrase of Saint Augustine, Saint Bernard says to us, in one of his sermons on various subjects:

> Stop to consider that *He is God*.[17] But, in order to arrive there you must first take care to see *who you are yourselves*, according to the word of the Prophet: "That men should know that they are men."[18] It is to that double consideration that your life ought to be consecrated, according to the word

15. Lk 18:1.
16. Mt 5:48.
17. Ps 46.
18. Ps 10.

of a saint in his prayer: "That I know myself, my God, and that I know you!"[19]

Here now is the phrase proclaimed by **William of Saint-Thierry**:

> Give attention to yourself—*vaca tibi*—; you yourself constitute abundant matter for solicitude for yourself.[20]

In his *Fourth Meditation*, he explains what he means by this attention to self which is not introspection at all. Withdrawn into solitude, he "is concerned to attend to himself"—*vaco vacare mihi*—; he recollects himself to ponder who he is and where he comes from: a creature made in the image of God; and that ends in knowing God, in attending to God, in occupying himself with God. These two poles are united: to know one's self and to know God; to know one's self in order to know God.[21]

Bernard dedicates a whole passage of his *Thirty-sixth Sermon on the Song of Songs* to the necessity of knowing yourself in order to know God. The soul which considers itself under God's gaze sees its misery; this is frightening, it would lead to despair, because in itself, around itself there is no means of escaping from it. Yes, but! There is one exit: divine mercy. Human misery, yes; but even stronger is God's mercy.

The knowledge of self, of your bottomless misery has been the means of knowing what God himself is: Goodness, Mercy, Love:

> In this way your self-knowledge will be a step to the knowledge of God.[22]

Having a solitary heart

Here we need only transcribe this impassioned supplication **William** makes in one of his meditations:

---

19. Bernard, Div 2.1.
20. William, Ep frat I.27; CF 12:46.
21. William, Med 4.8–9; CF 3:112,117.
22. Bernard, SC 36.5–6; CF 7:177–179.

Give me, O Lord, the comfort of my wilderness—a solitary heart and frequent communing with you.[23]

Intus—a hiding place—to descend into one's self—to shut one's self within self—to have a solitary heart,

in order to rest with God, *to speak with him.*

Speaking with God

Father François de Sainte Marie, in his little book *Being Present to God and to Self* (note these two elements which we find put side by side: God, self) has these simple but profound lines:

> Speech, much more than anything else, will be useful to us in keeping contact with God. It is the great resource of the blind for fostering a relationship. Like the gaze, speech goes in search of the other, draws his attention, obliges him to make a response. Now, the rules of dialogue are not destroyed in spirituality, although God there plays the role of a mute interlocutor. He sees us, but he remains silent. We are the blind ones who speak; he is the Seeing one who voluntarily keeps silence. Speech will serve more to draw our own attention than his: it will help us to truly enjoy his presence . . .
>
> Ejaculatory prayers are incessant efforts of the blind person who is in some ways afraid God will flee from him and who keeps up the conversation without ceasing, as if to say to him: "Are you still really there, my Beloved?"[24]

A text of **Gilbert of Hoyland** runs the same way. At least he begins with the same thought: we ought to speak to God, whom we cannot see, to make him hear our cry; it is a way of reaching him:

> To us you are darkness, to us inaccessible; inaccessible to our vision, yes, but not to our voice; for where reason does

23. William, Med 4.9; CF 3:115.
24. Fr François de Ste Marie, *Présence à Dieu et à soi-même.* (Paris, 1943), 20 and 22.

not reach, prayer penetrates. (Containing a play on words: *quo non approximat* ratio, *pertransit* oratio.)

This could be expressed in the form of a quick dialogue:

> "I can't see him!"
> "Well then, talk to him! And that will give you a contact, a certain vision."

Gilbert adds that the word, the cry launched toward God will be, will lead to a vision of God:

> "My cry in his sight," says the psalmist, "entered into his ears"—*clamor meus* in conspectu ejus *introivit* in aures ejus.[25] Therefore let our cry also enter into your sight, that you may emerge into our sight and even consent to be seen, though you do not permit our embrace.[26]

Isaac of Stella compares the soul to the boat on the lake, on the day of the storm. Jesus was there. Be careful not to let him sleep!

> Just you start sleeping to him, brothers, while he is speaking to you, and at that very instant he sleeps to you.[27]

Isaac wants us always to speak to Jesus, to listen to him, or to ask him questions.

This brings us back to saying again how necessary it is **to stay awake**.

Don't say to yourselves: "How complicated it is! It's necessary to be in the interior, to go down in, to shut myself there, it's necessary to hide myself, it's necessary to stay awake on top of all that!" No, clearly, it's all one thing, it is the same reality considered from different angles.

Keep watch. If you go to sleep in front of Jesus, he goes to sleep in front of you, and then comes the tempest, because the

---

25. Ps 17:7.

26. Gilbert, Tract 3.1; CF 34:23–24. This confusing switch from God as "him" to God as "you" is in the original.

27. Isaac, 4 p Epi 2; PL 194, 1736A; CF 11:115.

tempest, which represents all the malignant forces, doesn't sleep. Once again it is **Isaac** who says it in the same passage.

The guard of the heart

This word is biblical.[28] Our Fathers have used it. **Saint Bernard**, in his *Seventeenth Sermon on Various Subjects*, says that this guard of the heart consists in keeping watch over its affections and over its thoughts, thoughts which come, affections which occupy it. To achieve this, it is necessary to guard your hands and your lips.[29] His entire *Eighty-second Sermon* is also on this guard of the heart.

You need to struggle fiercely, to guard your heart like a fortress; it is besieged on all sides, and you have to rescue it, to take the appropriate means of liberating it.

These kinds of thoughts are distractions which are sometimes very persistent during prayer; they pester you. **William**, in his *Ninth Meditation*, shows that he was himself assailed, and had a hard time getting rid of this interior dance; but at last he arrived at serenity, at perfect calm.[30] In his *Golden Epistle*, his prayer is so disturbed by distractions that he sees them as the birds of prey that fastened on the sacrifice of Abraham.[31]

Baldwin of Ford groans: his prayer is nothing but a web of distractions . . .[32]

This is the atmosphere of the retreat, this is our everyday life: recollection, guarding the heart, living in ourselves, interior life, presence to God and to self.

28. Prv 4:23.
29. Bernard, Div 17.8.
30. William, Med 129–131; CF 3:145–148.
31. William, Ep frat I.16; CF 12:34.
32. Baldwin, Tract 3; CF 39:80.

II PASSING FROM SELF TO GOD

We now enter immediately into the theme of the retreat: passing from self to God. It can be expressed also in these different ways: to forget yourself, not to be concerned with self, to leave yourself aside or, to put it a bit informally, to let yourself fall; to ignore self, to deny self, to die to self. And all that corresponds to something very firmly positive, all that, in order to occupy yourself with God, to think about God, to be ravished by God, by what he is and by what he does, to bless him at all times, to praise him, to contemplate him. We feel it in advance: there is a whole gamut here; this "passage" has diverse intensities, manifestations, and expressions. The point is to ignore yourself as one ignores a person whom one does not know or whom one does not wish to know, to turn away from self, as soon as you notice that you are becoming the center of your interest. At certain moments, to struggle positively against yourself, against your bad nature, the old man, to lose yourself, to hate yourself, according to the words of Jesus in the gospel, in order to bring back, as much as is possible for [human] nature, but above all as is possible and even easy for the grace of God, to bring back all your attention, your intention (in the sense of tension, not of contention), all thought, all love toward and for God, toward and for Jesus, true God and true man, toward and for the Virgin Mary. She is the ideal creature, completely transparent, allowing herself to be pierced by the divine light without dimming it, without keeping any of it for herself, completely related to God, and she turns toward her Son and her God all who turn toward her.

It is clear that right now I could state the source of the ideas that I have found among our Fathers concerning this passing from self to God, and develop those ideas. First I would rather transcribe a dialog of Saint Francis of Assisi with Brother Leo, which expresses perfectly that practical way of passing from self to God, then I will permit myself to tell two experiences of my monastic youth which were beneficial to me; finally I will quote some passages from our Cistercian authors, arranged under a few titles.

1) Dialogue of Saint Francis with Brother Leo[1]

"Do you know, brother, what purity of heart is?"

"It is not having any fault with which to reproach oneself," responded Leo without hesitating.

"Then I understand your sadness," said Francis, "because one always has something about which to reproach himself."

"Yes," said Leo, "and it is precisely that which makes me despair of arriving one day at purity of heart."

"O, Brother Leo, believe me," responded Francis, "don't worry so much about the purity of your soul. Turn your gaze toward God. Admire him. Rejoice in what He is, He, all holiness. Thank him because of himself. Having a pure heart is exactly that, little brother.

"And when you are thus turned toward God, above all do not turn back to yourself at all. Don't ask where you stand with God. The sadness of not being perfect and finding yourself a sinner is still a human sentiment, too human. You must lift your gaze higher, much higher. There is God, the immensity of God and his unalterable splendor. The pure heart is the one which does not cease adoring the living and true Lord. It takes a profound interest in the very life of God and it is capable, in the midst of its miseries, of vibrating to the eternal innocence and to the eternal joy of God. Such a heart is at the same time overflowing and stripped. It is enough for it that God should be God. In that alone it finds all its peace, all its pleasure. And God himself is therefore all its holiness."

"God nevertheless demands our effort and our fidelity," observed Leo.

1. Éloi Leclerc, *Sagesse d'un pauvre.* 13e éd. (Paris, 1984) 113–116, with the kind permission of *Éditions franciscaines.*

"Yes, without a doubt," responded Francis. "But holiness is not an accomplishment of the self, nor a fullness which one gives oneself. It is first of all an emptiness which one discovers and accepts, and which God comes to fill in the measure that the person opens himself to His fullness.

"Our nothingness, you see, if it is accepted, becomes the free space where God is still able to create. The Lord does not allow his glory to be carried off by anyone. He is the Lord, the Unique, the only Holy. But he takes the poor person by the hand, he pulls him out of his mud, and makes him sit with the princes of his people, so that he may see His glory. God then becomes the jewel of his soul.

"To contemplate the glory of God, Brother Leo, to discover that God is God, eternally God, beyond what we are or can be, to rejoice fully in what he is, to be in ecstasy before his eternal youth and to thank him for himself, for his unfailing mercy, that is the most profound demand of that love which the Spirit of the Lord does not cease to pour into our hearts. That's what it is to have a pure heart.

"But this purity is not obtained by force of arms and by being grasping."

"How do you do it?" demanded Leo.

"It is necessary simply to keep nothing of yourself. Sweep out everything, even that sharp perception of our distress. Make a clean place. Accept being poor. Renounce everything that is heavy, even the weight of our faults. Have nothing more than the glory of God, become irradiated by it. God is, that is enough. The heart then becomes light. It no longer feels itself. It has abandoned every care, every inquietude. Its desire for perfection is changed into a simple and pure desire for God."

2) Two personal experiences

A very simple practice

When I was a novice, I often felt myself to be in good spiritual shape (at least so it seemed to me), and sometimes in much less good shape. Sometimes God seemed close to me, easy to reach, like a father, a friend, and sometimes far off, cold, almost as if avoiding me. I see again the place where, one day during work, I stopped and told myself, "God doesn't change; he isn't on good terms with me one day, and another day dissatisfied without good reason. Here's what I'm going to do: when things are going well, I will say to myself: 'It's not going better than when things are going badly,' and when things are going badly, I will say to myself, 'It's not going worse than when things were going well.' OK! Let's try it."

The first few days things went well and it wasn't difficult to say, "This isn't going better than when things are bad." But when several days later the wind changed and things went poorly, I wanted to stick to my resolution and, not without effort, I said to myself, "Things aren't going worse than the past few days; God hasn't changed, and I see nothing special on my part which could have offended him." That was beneficial to me, but especially when a bit later it once again seemed to me that everything was going well, it was still more beneficial and easier to say to myself, "Things aren't going better than when everything was going badly." My faith grew stronger.

This exercise having repeated itself a certain number of times, I realized because I had experienced it that God did not change at all and I didn't change either. I was still in reality a poor fellow whom God loved well (this shows progress in the knowledge of myself and of God). I experienced a great stability which seemed to me to resemble the eternity of God.

You can imagine my rapture when a while later, I happened on a passage of **Saint Bernard**, where I found this phenomenon perfectly described,[2] right down to the mention of that impression of eternity:

> You will ride above the vicissitudes of good and evil times
> with the poise of one sustained by values that are eternal,
> with that enduring, unshakeable equanimity of the man of
> faith who thanks God in every circumstance.

2. Bernard, SC 21.5–6; CF 7:7–8.

All the argumentation of the saint rested on a verse from Ecclesiasticus: "In the good days, don't be forgetful of the bad; and in the bad, don't be forgetful of the good."[3] Later I realized that more than once, **Saint Bernard** took up again that lesson of the Sage.[4]

In reality that grace was a light, a force which God gave me to get beyond my impressions, a form of secret attachment to myself, to go beyond myself, the fluctuating "me," to God who does not change, to God who considers me always with his faithful love, all poor and sinful as I am.

But the other grace was much more consequential. Since it seems to me that reporting it could be useful to more than one reader, permit me to explain it simply.

A liberating experience

The last six months of my novitiate were hard. During that time I experienced something which up to that point I had never experienced. That was the fact of living continually with an absolutely unbearable companion, and that companion was myself. Everywhere I found myself, even in the good actions where I had done my best to act with purity of intention, a voice seemed to whisper to me, "The others are going to think that you were charitable, that you accepted that humiliation well." It was impossible to escape from it. When I went to bed at night, I would say to myself, "At last, I will be rid of myself." And on waking, there was the same unbearable man whom I found again and who did not leave me the entire day.

Profession came. Nothing had changed. Then several days afterward, Father Godefroid Bélorgey, then prior of Scourmont, came to preach our annual retreat. He was a former cavalry officer who at the age of thirty was "converted," and gave himself to God with all his ardor. He didn't look very good-natured, but when he spoke of God in his talks, you saw his face light up. Rather than expounding on wise men, he brought his experience

3. Si 11:27.
4. So Bernard, Div 3.3; Circ 3.10, etc.

as a monk, as a man who lived in the presence of God, who could truly say, "Jesus in the Sacrament, the Holy Trinity in us, what does the rest matter to us?" Everything was brought back to one point: the presence of God, of a God who loves us tenderly. I drank in his words. I went to see him. Here is, I believe, a fairly accurate transcription of the conversation:

"My father, is it possible to forget oneself entirely, not to think of anything but God?"

"Why not?"

"I am a little afraid of illusion . . . ."

"I don't see anything of illusion in that; you have only to try it."

It was over and I left, but with an enormous joy—I could have danced in the corridor! A fantastic liberation: I now had my secret! I don't want to bother about myself anymore, to know what others think of me, what I think of myself, only GOD! GOD! GOD! He, Beauty which does not change, Goodness, Love! That was singing in my heart!

The office of Vespers came; I said to myself "I am going to heaven, with the Holy Virgin, the angels and the saints, to sing, to praise God," and that took me through all that office. And during the quarter hour of prayer that followed, I said to myself, "Let's just continue," and I repeated within myself several times *Gloria Patri* (where there is no question of anything but God, nothing of me). At collation (a light fast-day meal), taken in silence, head covered by the monk's hood, again: God! God! where in company with the Holy Virgin (which comes to the same thing), during this time of Advent, as though under her eye, eyes lowered, but as though facing her smile. And so it was until I went to bed. The next day, upon waking, in place of that unbearable man with whom to pass the day—God, that Father of goodness, that Jesus, that Virgin Mary . . . the company was very much sweeter. What is said of Wisdom in Scripture, was perfectly true of the Virgin Mary: "Life with her has no bitterness."[5]

A few days after the retreat, without having looked for anything, three thoughts rose in my heart, and I resolved to

5. Ws 8:16.

review them four times a day (upon waking, before the office of
Tierce, before the morning work, before the afternoon work) in
my spirit, in my head, without imposing formulas on myself, just
something spontaneous, more or less brief or developed:

> 1) My God, I don't want to be occupied with anything but
>   you, Beauty, Goodness!
> 2) I come to you like a small child: I will do my best, but it
>   is laughable; you alone can get me where I'm going.
> 3) I believe in your love for me, in your tenderness! I am
>   your beloved . . .

Well, it was a passage *from me* (even though it was for God
that I wanted perfection) *to God* (without being concerned even
with my perfection, but with Him!).

That lasted during many months; I don't say that I did not
commit some sins, but I saw them right away and, instead of
being cast down, or even made sad about turning back in upon
myself, I saw things from the other side, the side of God. For the
rest, completely, naturally, I developed a habit of often saying,
"My God, how does it look from your side?" (to appreciate
everything or live everything; how to attend Mass, how to judge
a brother or behave myself with him, etc.); even how to look at
myself and how to know myself; no introspection, but truly,
I believe, as **William of Saint-Thierry** says: "For the limits of
human imperfection are never better realized than in the light
of God's countenance."[6]

No one should believe that this spirituality is easy and
requires no effort; it is more apt to make the self die, to accept
not making self your center, to walk always at God's side. You
no longer know very much about yourself, but you know that
God is good, that He, He is worthy of being loved, and you say
the first part of the *Our Father* with fervor.

I will end this second point with two memories.

Two memories

In our third year in high school, we had a professor who had
a particular talent for drawing perfectly straight lines on the large

6. William, Ep frat II.18; CF 12:97.

blackboard. One day he said to us, "You ask yourselves how I can draw such straight lines? It's very simple! I put my chalk at point A, at the extreme lower left of the blackboard. Then, I no longer look at my fingers or at the chalk, but at the destination point B, at the top of the other end of the board, and the line is automatically straight." He was right, and it works the same way in the spiritual life: it is not yourself you ought to look at while acting, but God, and while we concern ourselves with him, he concerns himself with us. Besides, has he not said in the gospel, "You shall live *in me* and I *in you*"?

One evening, I was in conversation with my Father Abbot, Dom Chautard, when the warning sounded for Compline. We descended, and I followed him down the staircase. Turning back and prolonging the conversation, he said, "You see, my child, it's as it says in the psalm: 'My eyes are always turned toward the Lord, because he himself draws my feet from the net.' We must look at God, and he will make himself responsible for putting our feet where they ought to be, and for pulling them out of the net when needed."

Contemplation is looking at God and not at ourselves; contemplation makes us leave ourselves and not turn in upon ourselves.

3) Passages from Cistercian authors on this subject

Our Fathers love to trace spiritual itineraries, and they note this passage from self to God. One could arrange their texts fairly well under these three rubrics:

Being happy with God
You, not me
Disinterested love

Being happy with God

This expression is not opposed to "being happy with self," but to "trying to make God happy with me." Obviously, it is normal and often praiseworthy that we seek to please God. Jesus always did what was pleasing to his Father. But there can be, and even frequently is, a certain subtle self-seeking in it. We found it pointed out in the words addressed by Saint Francis of Assisi to Brother Leo. We want, in giving ourselves to God, to give him something "beautiful," of which we are secretly proud. Above *I am pleasing to God* is *God is pleasing to me*; or again, better than seeking to know if God is happy with me—which is often, let us repeat, very praiseworthy, when it is desired with purity of intention—is *being happy with God.*

Saint Bernard, in his *One Hundred Third Sermon on Various Subjects*, traces a spiritual itinerary. He reviews four stages:

—One begins by *loving one's own soul*; one loves oneself: one fears hell, one desires heaven.

—Afterwards, one *loves justice*, that is to say one faithfully does one's duty; one undergoes purifying trials which God sends to expiate one's sins.

—At the third stage, one is a *friend of Wisdom*, who says in a motherly way, "My child, give me your heart." *One tries to please God, that He may be content* with what one is or what one does.

—At the fourth, one *has become wise*; it is going beyond oneself. I no longer act so that God should be pleased with me, but because I am pleased with God.

> non ut Deo placeat
> sed quia placet ei Deus.[7]

That's what blessed Pierre le Borgne did, abbot of Igny, then of Clairvaux. He repeated ceaselessly, "I am happy with God!"

I note in passing that this theme is very close to those of *resting in God*, of *doing the will of God*, of *serenity* at which the soul arrives. In this same *Sermon One Hundred Three*, Bernard evokes all these themes following this gradation (at the summit of which is the fact of being content with God) as being almost synonyms:

> Whoever has arrived there can sing in total confidence and tranquillity of conscience that song of the Sage: "In all things I have sought *rest*, etc."[8] Because he has found rest in all things, he whom *God pleases in all things*, he who has

7. Bernard, Div 103.1–4.
8. Si 24:11.

learned not to bend (*incurvare*) the will of God to his own,
but *his own to that of God*. He *will dwell in the heritage of the
Lord*, according to what the same Lord promised him: "I
will give you the land where you sleep,"[9] that is to say, *that
rest* where you are come through your labors and through
my grace, I will make it *stable and perpetual* for you. If he
adds: "and to your race," we can understand this to mean
that that tranquillity is not assured only in this life, but also
to your race, that is to say that your works will obtain the
glorification of your body.[10]

Nevertheless when God is close, it is easy to be happy with
him, but when the impression is the contrary (and it can be
terribly strong when faith and hope are put to the test), there is
great merit in forgetting yourself, in passing from the side of God,
to find it sufficient for yourself that he should be God, and that
all will go well because of him. In the *Gloria Patri*, let us repeat,
it is not a question of us, and this praise is always true, whether
it is sunny or rainy . . .

Gilbert of Hoyland has a consoling word. He speaks to
some nuns:

> In a word, you have only one longing, that he may please
> you ever more! How much does one please, when one
> cannot please enough? By no means can you be pleasing
> to yourselves more than if he is pleasing to you.[11]

Phrased in another way:

> He is never so happy with you as when you are happy
> with him.

In my long ministry as confessor of nuns, it has happened
that more than once I have given this penance: say from time to
time during the day: "My God, I am not happy with myself, but
I am very happy with you."

There is a passage out of self, a passage from self to God.

9. Gn 28:13.
10. Bernard, Div 103.4. Emphasis added by Fr Thomas.
11. Gilbert, SC 19.2; CF 20:239.

Gilbert again, in his *Eleventh Sermon on the Song of Songs,* distinguishes three degrees of Sabbaths; the last is that same forgetfulness of self, and that contentment with God:

> If you are free (if you have some leisure, *si vacas*), you have a sabbath; if you are free and have eyes to contemplate the delights of the Lord (*si vacas et vides, et contemplaris delectationes Domini*), then your sabbath is "delightful and holy," a glorious sabbath of the Lord; a sabbath within a sabbath, that is freedom in freedom.[12]

Up to this point Gilbert has not yet announced more than two sabbaths, the second being that of the Lord, in which we participate. He now introduces an intermediate step, that in which one *seeks to please God.* The most elevated of the sabbaths is that in which *we seek to be happy because of God,* and *we forget ourselves.*

You, not me

A second idea or practice which I find among our Fathers, in the sense of going beyond yourself, is that which I will call **You, not me**: how to ignore self, but through going to him, the Lord.

Bernard recommends leaving ourselves to one side from time to time, to evade that atmosphere which clings to sinful man; this, in his *Second Sermon on Various Subjects*:

> Let us groan under this burden, brothers, and, weeping the present bitternesses, let us try to strip ourselves sometimes of ourselves, to launch our souls and fire off our hearts "in that which *is theirs*" (*in id quod suum est*), which is to them the sweeter the more natural it is. That is what the words mean: "Be still and know that I am God."[13]

The same recommendation is in the *Commentary on the Song of Songs.* In his *Eleventh Sermon,* he invites us with a great deal of conviction to get out of ourselves sometimes, of the thought

---

12. Gilbert, SC 11.5; CF 14:145.
13. Ps 46. Bernard, Div 2.8.

of our sins, of our indignity and misery, to leap toward God, to dwell on the memory of the divine kindness, of the goodness of God. With Dom Godefroid Bélorgey, I would prefer to say that it is necessary to do it *often*, and even why not *every time that we think of it*? It is to leave a place of misery to enter into the joy of our Lord and God:

> Those, however, who are employed in the work of thanksgiving are contemplating and thinking about God alone, and so they cannot help but dwell in unity. That which they do is good because they offer to God the glory that is most rightly his; and it is also pleasant, since of its very nature it gives delight (*jucundum quia delectat*).
>
> And for that reason my advice to you, my friends, is to turn aside occasionally from troubled and anxious pondering on the paths you may be treading, and to travel on smoother ways where the gifts of God are serenely savored, so that the thought of him may give breathing space to you whose consciences are perplexed. I should like you to experience for yourselves the truth of the holy Prophet's words: "Make the Lord your joy and he will give you what your heart desires."[14]

It's true: you can breathe then. You let every thing fall away, there is nothing more than God; what peace that gives! Mgr Saudreau, deaf in his old age, did not notice that while he prayed, everyone heard what he was saying to God. Therefore, the Sisters of the Good Shepherd of Angers (with what glee!) heard him always repeat the same formula during the course of his prayer: "My God and my all!—a short pause—and the rest I blow off." He passed from himself into God; it was truly the "You, not me," and all the peace which such an elevation was able to give him!

One could entitle the first tractate of **Gilbert of Hoyland** *Contemplation of God, the occupation that consists of resting in God*. It is a very beautiful tractate addressed to his friend Roger. He speaks above all of that occupation with heaven that is the praise of God without regard for oneself, because one has totally

---

14. Ps 37. Bernard, SC 11.2; CF 4:69–70.

passed into God. Already here below this occupation with God is possible; it is more valuable than being occupied with yourself, even though that is a good thing:

> It is unquestionably excellent to keep oneself unsullied and not to be "conformed to this world," but it is far superior to be reformed for the future world (*nec* conformari *huic sæculo; sed longe præstantius futuro* reformari, *et* transformari *a claritate in claritatem*) and to be transformed from one glory to a greater glory. To be unremitting in so looking out is to stand on the lookout of the Lord and to stand throughout the day.[15]

He wishes ardently to stay on the spot in which he contemplates God; he recognizes that it isn't by successive leaps that he can carry himself toward heaven; he lands there for an instant, then he falls back, like gymnasts who leap and fall back to earth each time.[16]

You, not me. In his *Third Tractate*, Gilbert has this very beautiful image, which expresses the experience of a mystic: God passes close to the soul; he draws it after him; he makes it pass into himself. These are three steps, and these words may cause us to reflect:

> *Pertransit a nobis,*
> *ut nos attrahat post se,*
> *et transire faciat ad se.*[17]

Our Fathers willingly quoted, among other phrases from Psalm 71, the one which expresses the desire to be occupied only with God, with his holiness, not to be absorbed with our own holiness, still less with the consideration of our malice or of our personal insufficiency: *Lord, I will no longer remember anything but your justice alone.* Thus this passage from **Guerric**, taken from a sermon for Christmas:

> Lord, I will remember your justice alone. In no wise will I remember my own justice, so as to exaggerate my labors,

15. Gilbert, Tract 1.2; CF 34:5.
16. Gilbert, Tract 1.3; CF 34:5.
17. Gilbert, Tract 3.7; CF 34:29.

make much of my merits; rather I will remember your justice alone who did freely bind yourself to me by your promise. . . . Therefore he conducts his case prudently before God who, reckoning nothing of his own justice, commits everything to mercy.[18]

Self-forgetfulness in order to think of nothing but God; to efface his *me* before the *You* addressed to God, **Baldwin** says it also in his way:

> "My soul has cleaved to you."[19] . . . and preferred you to itself; it has neglected itself for you, so that it may love you more than itself.[20]

Here is the very literal translation which, inelegant as it may be, speaks more plainly. You will notice all the *you*s, in order to put them forward: he alone counts! All the *self*s which are equivalent to *me*, to put them behind:

> My soul is linked *behind you*,
> putting *before self, you*,
> putting *self behind you*,
> in order to love *you more than self*.

Saint Bernard, in his *Eighth Sermon on Various Subjects*, speaks of the soul that no longer asks anything for itself; it does not ask for anything but God himself. The sermon describes the stages of the spiritual life. At the fourth level we find the son, and at the fifth the spouse:

> The soul has learned, by a frequently-repeated experience, that the Lord is good to those who hope in him, to the soul which seeks him; so well that it is from the intimacy of his heart, from the depths of his conscience, that this man cries out: "What is there for me in heaven, and of you what have I desired on earth? My flesh and my heart have fainted, O Lord, God of my heart, and my portion for eternity."[21]

18. Guerric, Nat 4.2; CF 8:57.
19. Ps 63.
20. Baldwin, Tract 4; CF 39:116.
21. Ps 73.

It is no longer her personal advantage, it is no longer her own happiness, nor her own glory, nor anything similar which the soul has arrived at this point looks for, as if she still loved herself, but she is completely stretched out towards God, she no longer has anything but a sole and perfect desire, which is that the King should enter his tent, so that she may attach herself to him and take pleasure in him.[22]

John of Ford, that great English mystic, still so little known, having arrived at the end of the Song upon which he had commented, thinks that the last words, "You who live in the gardens," are the shafts which the Bridegroom fires at his beloved, and which inflict on her a wound which pierces her heart and keeps her captive; it is an invasion by the love of Christ: *he conquers the place*:

> The arrow . . . of love . . . [which pierces her soul] never comes back. . . . No, it pierces firmly into her very depths, reaching even to the division of the joints and the marrow. In fact, it renders all the bride's will and intellect captive, so that *there is absolutely nothing left in her over which the love of Christ has not triumphed.*[23]

In a much earlier sermon, the Eighth, John has an admirable passage where he begins to speak in the first person of his soul which he calls "a small poor girl" (*paupercula*); her righteousness is nothing: there are some foul rags; but her true righteousness is that of Christ, a magnificent cloak which covers her, which belongs to her in all truth. She can no longer remember anything but the righteousness of Jesus. It would be worth reproducing the whole passage, but here are only a few lines of it:

> So I will wrap myself in it with perfect confidence. It has come to me from heaven, falling to my lot as one who has complete belief in him who justifies the ungodly.[24] If you are to judge me, O my Lord, if the Father has really put all

---

22. Bernard, Div 8.9.
23. John of Ford, SC 118.1; CF 47:218–219.
24. Rom 4:5.

judgement into your hands, then see how your justice, by your free gift, is my justice.[25]

He is no longer going to think of himself, he is going to forget himself, he is going to throw himself onto God:

> I will remember only [your own justice], and throwing myself onto it, I will not be ashamed. And so, if you judge me, I beg you, judge me according to this justice that is in me. With that to cover me, I will not fear when winter comes, or the heat of summer. Instead, I will glory, because the Lord has clothed me with the garment of salvation, has covered me with the robe of righteousness.[26]

Here is an experience and a spiritual doctrine completely sure, which we have already found, and very strongly, in Saint Bernard, that is the conviction that one has nothing good in oneself, but God, or Christ, as Saint Paul says, gives us his own righteousness.[27] We rest on it with total confidence. **Bernard** goes so far as to say:

My merit therefore is the mercy of the Lord. Surely I am not devoid of merit as long as he is not [devoid] of mercy. And if the Lord abounds in mercy, I too must abound in merits.[28]

In the same sense, he says that knowledge of himself was for him a step toward knowing God: seeing his misery made him aware of the only issue to come out of it: he understood the mercy of God; he met God who is Mercy.[29]

Allusion has already been made to that important text.[30]

William of Saint-Thierry, in his *Life of Saint Bernard*, reports the following extremely significant anecdote:

> One time the Man of God was ill, with a stream of phlegm flowing almost ceaselessly from his mouth. His body, drained of strength, was failing and he had all but come to

25. John of Ford, SC 8.6; CF 29:169.
26. John of Ford, SC 8.6; CF 29:169–170.
27. 1 Cor 1:30.
28. Bernard, SC 61.5; CF 31:144.
29. Bernard, SC 26.6; CF 7:5–6.
30. In chapter 1. Bernard, SC 36.5–6; CF 7:179.

his last. Accordingly, his sons and friends gathered round, as if for the obsequies of so great a Father. I too was there with the rest, since his kindness counts me too among his friends.

When it seemed to him he was drawing his very last breath, then in an ecstasy of his mind, he had a vision: in it he was himself being presented before the tribunal of the Lord. Satan too was on hand, as adversary, pressing hard his damnable accusations.

Once Satan had had his full say for the prosecution, the Man of God was allowed his say. Then, not at all terrified or even disturbed, he said: "I admit that I am not myself worthy; nor can I, by any merits of my own, lay claim to the Kingdom of Heaven. Nevertheless, there is a double claim to it on the part of my Lord, by inheritance from his Father and by merit of what he suffered. Since he contents himself with the first claim, he concedes the other to me. Acting on that gift, I unabashedly vindicate to myself the Kingdom of Heaven."

Abashed rather was his foe at such a word and the tribunal session was dissolved. The Man of God came back to himself.[31]

Let's return to **Gilbert**, to find a teaching on the passage from self to God, on that effacement of myself, in order that **You**, the Christ, alone may have the place. It is a summit of the spiritual ascent. Gilbert distinguishes in his *Second Sermon on the Song* three sorts of little beds:

> in the first, the Bride is close to herself, or at home: this little bed is hers.
> in the second, the Bridegroom is close to her, in her home; the little bed belongs to both of them.
> In the third, there is nothing more than him![32]

You may find that I insist a great deal on this phenomenon of the spiritual life, on the passage from self to God, but that is so important in sanctification. It is a secret of holiness; we will

31. William, Vita Bern; *Vita Prima*, 70.
32. Gilbert, SC 2.4; cf. CF 14:59.

soon show it with the aid of formal words of saints or of the holy people of our times, but already those old monks of Cîteaux had understood it, their spirituality was *paschal*: it was a matter of nothing less than entering into the mystery of Christ, of taking part in his death and in his resurrection.

William of Saint-Thierry speaks, in his *Commentary on the Song*, of those "poor in spirit" who are all filled with the Spirit of the Lord. Here is the entire passage which we touched upon lightly at the beginning of these chats:

> The Hebrews (that is, they who pass over), knowing that they had been saved by you from the destroyer (which is the meaning of the name "Pharaoh") and from the region of darkness (which is Egypt), in the shedding of blood and the sacrament of the Paschal Lamb, celebrate in haste the Pasch, that is the Passover of the Lord, by passing from vice to virtue, from the things of time to the things of eternity, from earth to heaven, from themselves to God, while the sins and vices that pursued them are drowned in the waters reddened by the blood of the Lamb. In adversity, as in the terror of the night, they have for light, like the pillar of fire, the fire and strength of the Holy Spirit; but in prosperity, as in daylight, they have the power of the Most High overshadowing them like the cloud.[33]

One could cite many more texts on the "weakening of self," and the corresponding invasion of Christ. So as not to go on indefinitely, let's quote two last ones, one from Gilbert, the other from Aelred.

Commenting on the phrase in the Song: "My soul has melted, since my Beloved has spoken," **Gilbert** explains this *melting* thus:

> O wonderful power of the word so passionately burning! It sets the heart on fire, converts the loins, reduces the soul to nothing in its own sight in comparison with God, makes the soul melt and run from self, so that the soul is no longer with self but as the psalmist continues: "I am always with You." Therefore the soul is neither in herself nor with herself but with her God.[34]

33. William, Cant 5.68; CF 6:55.
34. William, Cant 44.7; CF 26:535.

Here now is the text, the prayer of **Aelred** in which he desires ardently "to weaken/faint" from self:

> My soul, . . . be like a broken shard,
> so that by abandoning yourself and passing wholly to God,
> you may know how to live and die
> not for yourself
> but only for him
> who died and rose again for you.[35]

A secret of perfection

It is a considerable matter to forget oneself in order to occupy oneself with God; it is a secret of perfection, of union with God, of contemplation. Here are several testimonies of authors more or less recent:

Marie-Antoinette de Geuser, whom Father Plus formerly made known under the name of **Consummata**, said: "I want to be the small one occupied by the great forgotten one." She said again:

> The simplest way is to look at nothing but him; in a short time he does great things.

Blessed Elisabeth of the Trinity speaks explicitly of *secret*:

> Yes, I believe it, *the secret* of peace and of happiness is to forget self, to cease to occupy oneself with self.

Brother Laurence of the Resurrection, simple Carmelite lay brother of the seventeenth century, based his entire spirituality on the practice of the presence of God, a practice that consisted in leaving himself in order to occupy himself with God.

In an intimate prayer of Father Auguste Valensin, which he wanted read as his corpse was lowered into the grave, one finds these words which speak well of the **You** of God and of the **Me** of the man who recognizes that he is poor, insignificant but loved:

35. Aelred, Mir; PL 195, 520A; CF 17:113–114. Italics in psalm quotation from English edition removed.

O my God, keep me from considering myself, since it is your love which it is necessary to gaze on, it alone, unmerited like all love.

Why does God love me? Certainly not for what I am. Then, what good does it do for me to mope about what I am? He loves me, because he is **Love**, and I have nothing to value, I have nothing to do: I only have to allow myself to be loved, saying to my Father that, for **Myself**, I want to love **Him**, as He wants to be loved; and that I ask him to love himself in **Me** by **Me**.[36]

What we find in these modern spiritual people, this doctrine, and above all this practice of self-forgetfulness, in order to occupy oneself as far as possible with nothing but God, we find abundantly in our Fathers. Numerous texts have been quoted on this aspect: *to be content with God*: it matters little whether one is content with oneself. Numerous texts have also been quoted on that other aspect of the same truth: *You, not me*. It remains for us to look at this third aspect: disinterested love.

Disinterested love

Love is, of itself, *ecstatic, centrifugal*. It makes one leave self and live in the loved one. That is what Saint Augustine meant by saying that the one who loves lives more in the one loved than in himself. Intelligence draws into self, reduces to its own level of immateriality that which it knows; what one knows of the infinitely greater than self, God, one reduces in knowing it, one expresses it by concepts; in the same way, if one knows the smallest of beings, one expresses them in concepts, which is to make them larger. Intelligence draws the object into itself, assimilates it, changes it in some sort, and it is in changing it that it knows it. Love follows an inverse process: it carries itself towards its object; it goes to find it as it is. It becomes more noble in loving something greater than itself, becomes more vile in loving something viler than itself. When it is a question of an

---

36. Auguste Valensin, *La joie dans la foi* (Paris: Éditions Montaigne, 1954) 106.

authentic love, one loves in a disinterested manner: one desires the good, the happiness of the loved one more than one's own.

Here is how **Aelred** defines or describes love. This passage is borrowed from the *Mirror of Charity*:

> What is love?
> Unless I am mistaken, love is a wonderful delight of the spirit:
> all the more attractive because more chaste;
> all the more gentle, because more guileless;
> and all the more enjoyable because more ample.
> It is the heart's palate which tastes that you are sweet,
> the heart's eye which sees that you are good.
> And it is the place capable [of receiving] you, great as you are.
> Someone who loves you grasps you.
> The more one loves the more one grasps, because you yourself are love,
> for you are charity.
> This is the abundance of your house,
> by which your beloved will become so inebriated that,
> *quitting themselves, they will pass into you.*
> And how else, O Lord, but by **loving you?**[37]

Gilbert says that love is a drunkenness, a sleep *which tears the soul from itself,* and does not permit it to stay with itself.[38]

When love attains a certain degree, one loves much more for the other than for self. The lovableness of the other seduces so much that one wishes to love nothing except him, because he is worthy of being loved. One understands how much all that is worth, above all the love for God. How many times **William** repeats that our love is not made except for God, that one should love nothing but God or in God, for God. To cite only one text, here is what one reads in his book *On Contemplating God*:

> Then to want you, to want you vehemently—that is, to love
> you and to love you exclusively, for you will not tolerate
> being loved along with any other thing whatever, carnal
> or spiritual, earthly or heavenly, that is not loved for your
> sake—to want you thus is to want nothing but what is good;

---

37. Aelred, Mir I.1; PL 195, 505 B–C; CF 17:88.
38. Gilbert, SC 42.1; CF 26:504.

and that is tantamount to having all one wants. For everyone possesses you just insofar as he loves you.[39]

Then we understand phrases like those of **Gilbert**:

> O how shameless and ungrateful am I, if I do not love such a one (*si non ego talem diligam*). . . . I will love you, sweet Lord, *if not for myself, at least for yourself,* that I may satisfy your desire.[40]

Guerric has, among other admirable sermons, the First for Easter which deserves to be transcribed and explicated almost line by line. Let us content ourselves with a rapid glance and the quotation of a few sentences. The holy abbot begins by pretending to speak of something other than the Resurrection, than of Jesus brought back to life. He takes in effect the text from Genesis: "They announced to Jacob: Joseph is alive! At this news, his spirit took on new life, and he said: if Joseph my son is alive, that is enough for me: I will go see him before I die."[41]

The monks must have looked a bit uncomfortable, because Guerric interprets their thoughts like this:

> "Very good, but what is the point of that? Has this any connection with today's joy and the triumph of Christ's resurrection? Remember that it is Paschal time. Are you going to feed us with Lenten fare again? Our soul hungers for the Paschal Lamb, the one for whom it has prepared itself by fasting all this time. Our heart is burning within for Jesus. It is Jesus we desire even if we do not yet merit to see him or listen to him. It is Jesus we are hungering for, not Joseph; the Redeemer, not the dreamer; the Lord of heaven, not of Egypt. Not the one who fills the belly, but he who nourishes the mind, the hungry mind."[42]

Guerric amuses himself thus for a moment, then he declares to his monks that it is a trap! It is indeed of Jesus that he intends

---

39. William, Contemp 11; CF 3:56.
40. Gilbert, SC 20.10; CF 20:260.
41. Gn 45:26–28.
42. Guerric, Pasc 1.1; PC 27, 37–39; CF 32:80.

to speak, and it is of Jesus that one must say: if Jesus lives, that is enough for me! What a beautiful sentence he has then, a sentence that calls out to us still today:

> By this token you may clearly know that your soul lives again fully in Christ if it echoes this sentiment: "It is enough for me that Jesus is still alive."[43]

He develops his subject, and how profoundly he is seized by it, he speaks of himself, confides in us, reveals to us the depths of his soul. There are steps, a progression in that love for Jesus which become more and more disinterested:

1) If he is alive, I am alive also;
If he lives, I live, since my soul is suspended from him;
yes, since he himself is my life,
he is all my reason for being.
This is already a very pure love, but Guerric does not neglect his own personal advantage: *I am alive*, because Jesus is alive.
2) What more could I want, if Jesus is alive?

I can lack nothing: Jesus is so much my good that if he is alive, the rest matters little to me, I want nothing more. This is a love which has progressed in purity, it seems: my true and only good is Jesus, Jesus alive, but I still see that *it is a good for me*, and I am not unaware of it.

3) Still better: even if I lose all the rest, that which touches me is unimportant, provided that Jesus is alive!

A love much more detached from self. "Even if I lose all the rest." It is almost a wish to lose all the rest, provided that he, he should be happy, he should be alive.

4) If it should be his good pleasure may I come to lack even myself, because, provided that he be himself, that is enough for me![44]

---

43. Guerric, Pasc 1.5; PC 27, 53; CF 32:84.
44. Guerric, Pasc 1.5; PC 27, 53; CF 32:84.

There, we are at the highest step. It is supreme disinterestedness, with no further regard for self, but rather one can envisage even giving up one's own self.

There is what love does: it pushes the "self" always farther out, and "He," he takes over the whole space. That makes me dream of the word of Isaiah:

> The space is too narrow for me, make room for me so that I may move in![45]

Finding oneself again in God

To pass into God; to forget self; to be content with God, and so much the worse for me! You, not me; to lose oneself; disinterested love: we have covered all that more or less.

We add that if you lose yourself in passing from self to God, here is where, without having explicitly looked for it, *you find yourself again in God*. This is experienced. You find in God, and only in him, your true face. The more you are supernatural, the more you are natural, your true self.

Baldwin has a few lines on this subject, putting everything into a theological plan, in the economy of salvation:

> At first, man is not in accord with reason. He retreats, as it were, from himself and begins to be robbed of the possession of his own land. [He begins] to be in exile within himself, just as if he were outside himself, in a strange land, in a land of forgetfulness, in the region of unlikeness. But when he returns to his heart after his transgression, he then finds himself near to himself, and he himself *is returned to himself* lest he be absent from himself. Then, just as in the Year of Jubilee, his possession is restored to him so that he may rest under his own vine and under his own fig-tree and possess the earth in peace, since he is meek. "Blessed are the meek, for they shall possess the land."[46]

45. Is 49:20.
46. Mt 5:4. Baldwin, Tract 9.2; CF 41:32–33.

A passage from **Gilbert**, in his *Commentary on the Song of Songs*, can seem a bit mysterious, but basically it is the point which interests us here which he draws attention to. A part of the soul, of its beauty, escapes from it, but not from Jesus. It is, so to speak, a treasure, belonging to the soul, which the Lord keeps himself; in renouncing it, the soul has acquired it, and it is the soul which gives it to itself:

> "My frame was not hidden from you," says the psalmist, "when I was being made in secret."[47] Though it be hidden from me, it is not hidden from you, for your "Spirit searches everything" even what is hidden in me. Would that I might have many such gifts hidden in me, known to you, good Jesus, and stored among your treasures. Perilous it is to store them in my understanding; therefore I entrust them more safely to yours. Yet it is not so much I who entrust them to you as you who do not entrust them to me. In your keeping you cherish still more safely what you have made in secret.[48]

Let us recognize that what Gilbert puts into relief here above all, is the secret of the soul which God keeps for her, all the spiritual goods which she has acquired which she does not really need to have knowledge of. But there is also this aspect of transformation: Jesus has worked in her, it is his own work, and at the same time it is indeed the soul that has become this thing: *she has become herself*, without really being aware of it. There is nonetheless, as I have said, something that happens during that transformation: one has lost self for Christ Jesus; one finds self again in Christ Jesus.

47. Ps 139:15.
48. Gilbert, SC 25.3; CF 20:309.

III RESTING YOUR SOUL

When you pass from self to God, you change your center of gravity, you find your true center: God. Made by God, according to the famous saying of Saint Augustine, we do not find rest until we have found God and rest ourselves in him. Otherwise, our heart is "un-quiet," agitated, instead of being tranquil.

You have left yourself to one side, effaced yourself before God, and behold in losing yourself to make room for him, you find yourself in him. It is good to be with God: everything in us then is well in place; before, it was dislocated.

We see it is not a matter of pure rest, a perfect "otium." There are inevitably some labors, multiple occupations, and even preoccupations which make demands on us, but we will have occasion to insist on this point: it is a great thing, which needs a true ascesis and a singular grace of God, to arrive at *seeking and even finding rest in all things*. You will perhaps have recognized here a biblical expression, often repeated in the liturgy with regard to the Holy Virgin: "In all things I have sought rest." **Baldwin of Ford** has a complete tractate, the Fifth, on this word from Sirach.[1]

William, the intimate friend and confidant of **Bernard**, was surely not making things up when he indicated the reasons which pushed the man of God [Bernard] to become a monk, and to deliberately choose the monastery of Cîteaux to execute his project:

> He saw that, while outwardly the World and its Prince had much to offer him: great wealth and hopes even greater (albeit all deceptive, vanities of vanities and all of them

1. Baldwin, Tract 5; CF 39:130–151.

vanity), inwardly he could hear Truth in Person crying
out constantly and saying: Come to me, all you who labor
and are burdened, and I shall refresh you. Take my yoke
upon you and *you shall find rest for your souls.*[2] Thus his
deliberation on the best, most perfect way to abandon the
world, *changed into a searching inquiry for a place where he
could find that rest for his soul under that yoke of Jesus Christ,
and find it in its most perfect purity.*

In his inquiry, he met up with Cîteaux, a new implantation
of a renewed monastic observance . . . .[3]

Don't think that these words are nothing but a piece of
literature; don't think either that this was an idea, a youthful
craze and that with experience Bernard recognized that rest
wasn't so much a fact for monks, that they were on the contrary,
rough workers, above all with all the foundations which needed
great devotion [to duty], and left only a bit of contemplative
leisure. No, this was an idea well anchored and well built up
in the spirit of the saint: the monk ought to seek rest, and it is
normal that he should find it.

In the *Forty-sixth Sermon on the Song*, concerning the little
bed covered with flowers, he raised his thought to the economy
of the Church. Previously, it was to monks that he assigned the
function of resting:

> And indeed in the Church the "bed" where one reposes is,
> in my opinion, the cloisters and monasteries, where one
> lives undisturbed by the cares of the world and the anxieties
> of life.[4]

He characterizes, a bit farther on, each of the functions of
the Christians in the Church: the prelates exercise authority; the
clerics enjoy a certain dignity; the Christian people distinguishes
itself by its sense of discipline, *and the monks by their peacefulness*
(*populi disciplinam, monachorum quietem*).[5]

---

2. Mt 11:28–29.
3. William, Vita Bern; *Vita Prima*, 13. Emphasis added by Fr Thomas.
4. Bernard, SC 46.2; CF 7:241.
5. Bernard, SC 46.4; CF 7:243.

When he comments on the verse of the Song: "If you do not know yourself, leave here!" Bernard takes it to mean that the Bridegroom reproaches the Bride for having gone out of herself, for not having rested within, and here is how he characterizes that leaving:

> from the spirit to the flesh, from things that are the soul's delight to desire of earthy pleasures, from the inward repose of the mind to the world's clattering bustle where worry allows no peace . . . .[6]

Saint Bernard has an admirable word:

> God is tranquil, he makes all tranquil,
> and looking on the Rested One is to be at rest.[7]
> *Tranquillus Deus, tranquillat omnia,*
> *et Quietum aspicere, quiescere est.*

You see that the translation given is very literal! But it was necessary for it to be so, to respect the vigor of thought and the alliterations, the assonances; in Latin nevertheless it is almost a song, it is inimitable!

Gilbert also has a word which concerns this:

> Only with a calm mind
> can one seek the delight of wisdom [(let us say seek God)], for with a restless gaze one cannot focus upon her.[8]

Thus, linking these two texts together:

> One holds his soul as tranquil as possible
> and one looks at God;
> and He who is tranquil, rested,
> He makes tranquil, rests the soul.

---

6. Bernard, SC 35.1; CF 7:165.
7. Fr Thomas does not provide a reference for this citation.
8. Gilbert, SC 1.2; CF 14:45.

Looking for rest in all things

Our Fathers who were great contemplatives, and loved to keep their souls tranquil before God, savored this verse of Sirach, which we have already pointed out:

> "In everything I have sought rest, and I will wait in the inheritance of the Lord."[9]

Guerric, in his *Third Sermon for the Assumption*, stresses this text, and develops the theme of spiritual rest throughout all his sermon.

He begins by this remark to which everybody willingly subscribes:

> Rest is welcome to the weary.

Then, he adds:

> Therefore while we celebrate the rest of God's holy Mother not only may our bodies be refreshed by this rest of a day from the work of the harvest but also our hearts may draw breath in remembrance and love of that eternal rest.[10]

Two verbs should be noted: *to breathe* (*respirare*) and *to be restored* (*recreari*). In that leisurely feast, where the soul rejoins the Virgin Mary who has entered into the rest of heaven, our bodies will be restored and our hearts where our souls take breath will breathe. There above, remarks Guerric, there will still be a need to harvest, but it will not be a labor:

> Yet there too, brethren, there too you will reap, but it is rest you will reap, you who are now sowing the work of this harvest.

He invites us then to rest under the wings of Jesus:

> O you who toil, O you who bear the day's burden and its heat; in the shade of Jesus' wings you will find rest for your

---

9. Si 24:12.
10. Guerric, Asspt 3.1; CF 32:179.

souls, firm support, shelter when the hot wind blows, shade
at noonday.

These are images to show that in coming to take refuge
near Jesus, one gives peace to the soul: worries, temptations fall
away . . .

Guerric goes on:

> Happy is he who in all his labors (*laboribus*)
> and in all his ways (*viis*)
> seeks blessed rest (of God),
> always hastening . . . to enter into that rest.[11]

A monk is mortified, he "afflicts his body," and takes pains
to live in peace with his brothers:

> Giving the preference, where his will is concerned,
>   to the rest and the
>   leisure of Mary,
>   to the extent that necessity demands
> he accepts the toil and the business of Martha.[12]

You see here that attitude which Guerric wants to find
among his monks: by taste, they ought to desire the rest of prayer,
of contemplation; but they are in a community, so it is needful
to know how to sacrifice their tastes, even spiritual ones, and
to devote themselves to the brothers. This double attitude is
also valuable for lay people in their family or social milieu. We
must not forget that Guerric is one of the rare ones, among the
Cistercian mystics, who had the grace of living long years under
the direction of Saint Bernard, who was able to profit from his
teaching, from his example, from his formation.

When we turn to the *Fiftieth Sermon on the Song of Songs* of
Bernard, we find again the same teaching: in the "order" to keep
concerning charity, although in the heart it is necessary to prefer
the "affective" charity, that intimate union of the soul with God—
it is, in the best sense of the word, the affective love—in practice
it is often necessary to give first place to "effective" charity, that
which is demonstrated in works, in devoting ourselves to others,

---

11. Guerric, Asspt 3.1; CF 32:179–180.
12. Guerric, Asspt 3.1; CF 32:180. The gospel for this feast was that of Mary
and Martha.

in service. We could write a book on this *action–contemplation* problem among the Cistercian spiritual people.

Guerric goes on:

> Yet [he] does this with as much peace and quiet of spirit as he can, and always brings himself back from that manifold distraction to the *one thing necessary.*[13]

There is a major theme for our Fathers, there something like a pillar of their spirituality, there a keystone of the edifice by which everything is bound together and mounts toward the unity of God, until grace can do no more than make us one with God:

To turn without ceasing, to pass from the multiple to the one (unity).

We will come back to this at greater length.

A man of this sort is at rest
even when he is working,
just as on the contrary the godless man has to work
even when he is resting. . . .
Just as happens in nature,
whatever is outside the simplicity and unity of a point
is in movement and agitation;
any circle whirls around all the faster
the further it is from the immobility of its principle, from its
axle, its center.
Truly the godless walk around in circles . . .
and therefore they cannot enter into that interior and
eternal rest.[14]

---

13. The French here has "Mais alors il se livre à ses affaires," with a note: *Negotium*, the opposite of *otium*. Note that the more important word is the positive *otium*, rest, leisure; *negotium* (the source of the French word *négoce* [business] is less valuable: it is a negative, the negation of a good. Obviously, *otium* is bad if it consists of inertia, of idleness (*otiositas*). William is indignant at those who condemn contemplation as idleness; it is, on the contrary, "the most important business" (*negotium negotiorum*), the supreme activity (Ep frat I.21; CF 12:39).

14. Guerric, Asspt 3.2; CF 32:180–181.

This reminds me very much of what **William** says in his *Eleventh Meditation*: it is necessary to center your action, center yourself well in God; then the circle of the action will be perfect.[15]

Guerric goes on, showing men who are practically atheists, "God-less," unhappy, broken; they have not known the road of peace, and that:

> because they have not even sought for it, so as to be able to say: "In all I sought rest," that is, in the midst of their manifold activity by which they are harassed and harass others to have in mind and to seek after *the one thing necessary*.

The just say:

> "**One thing** have I asked the Lord, this will I seek!"[16]

Reciprocal rest

Now,[17] Guerric asks: "Who [is it] principally who says 'In all I sought rest'?" He responds:

Wisdom (she searches for rest in the souls)
the Church
every faithful soul

There is in effect a reciprocal rest: the soul, the Virgin above all, rests in God—but God, Wisdom, rests also in the soul, in the Virgin above all:

> He will recall to you amid embraces and kisses, if I am not mistaken, how pleasantly he rested in the tent of your body, how with greater delight he dwelt in the inner chamber of your heart. . . . Blessed is he with whom God has found rest if but once, in whose tent he has rested if only for one hour.[18]

15. William, Med 11:13; CF 3:164–165.
16. Guerric, Asspt 3.2; CF 32:181.
17. Guerric, Asspt 3.3; CF 32:181.
18. Guerric, Asspt 3.3; CF 32:182. Emphasis in both sections added by Fr Thomas.

We point out in passing that it is always necessary to pay great attention when one of our Fathers employs an expression of this type: "just one time in his life." It is a matter then of a signal favor of God and something there is reason to beg for insistently: we must not miss that opportunity![19]

Jesus must find his rest in us. In fact, that attracts us! To rest in God, and God resting in us. It is correlative, just as:

> God content with us, and us content in God
> Jesus sleeps in front of us, if we sleep in front of him.

Jesus is like a vagabond, a poor wanderer—*vir vagus, et quasi viator declinans ad manendum*—. He asks for a resting place, he has nowhere to lay his head,[20] he stands at the door,[21] his head drenched with dew[22]—observe all those scriptural texts which show through—. It is necessary to open to him:

> Unless he finds with us the rest he is seeking,
> we shall not find in him the rest we desire.[23]

Here is the end of Guerric's sermon, where he gathers together all the teaching that he has given:

> Let us all then together so make a point of being quiet
>   that in our quiet
> we may always be occupied with meditation on eternal quiet,
>   and for desire of it be found ready for every work.
> May the blessed Mother of God, whose rest we are celebrating,
>   obtain this for us by her prayers
> from him who rested in the tabernacle of her body and her heart.
>   **He is eternal rest,**
>   Christ Jesus, to whom be honor and glory
>   for ever and ever. Amen.[24]

19. So Bernard, SC 6.8; CF 4:36; SC 35.1; CF 7:166; SC 69.7; CF 40:34; SC 83.6; CF 40:186; John of Ford, SC 19.1; CF 39:60.
  20. Mt 8:20.
  21. Acts 3:20.
  22. Sg 5:2.
  23. Guerric, Asspt 3.4; CF 32:182.
  24. Guerric, Asspt 3.6; CF 32:185. Emphasis added by Fr Thomas.

A tractate on rest

Baldwin of Ford devoted a tractate to the subject of rest. It is an exposition wound around the text from Sirach which Guerric just commented on: "In all things I have sought rest." The author puts this phrase into the mouth of God, into that of Christ, into that of the disciple of Christ, particularly into that of the monk, one after the other. Original and enriching insights are not lacking.

God, being himself his own rest, does not have to look elsewhere. Nevertheless, in all his works, he has desired to seek rest, especially in the creation of man: *rest for him*, and *rest for man*:

> In everything that God has done for us
> since the creation,
> he sought rest for himself in us,
> and [rest] for us in him.[25]

If man bends himself to the commandments of God, He will come to live in him, and the reverse is also true:

> When someone who is just has turned to God, God, by grace, dwells and rests within him, so that by receiving his commands with reverence and being obedient to him, he might, through obedience, be worthy to rest [in God]. The rest we desire is prepared by obedience to his commands.[26]

It can happen that in a monastic community—it is composed of men, and everyone agrees with Montaigne in admitting that "everywhere there are men, there are human foibles"—that certain brothers are difficult to tolerate. You don't have to think that it is necessary to wait until such a brother has been called home by God, or until he should have left the community, to find the peace of soul which everyone wants. Baldwin thinks, on the contrary, that the brother who gives exercise to the others, ought to be an occasion of peace for those around him:

25. Baldwin, Tract 5; CF 39:131.
26. Baldwin, Tract 5; CF 39:139.

> For it often happens that when good and wicked are living
> together communally, the wicked are reformed, and the
> good become better and purer. The lily springs up among
> thorns, and the just man grows among the wicked like a
> lily. He is pricked by the spines and suffers tribulation at
> the hands of the wicked, just as Jacob [did] at the hands
> of Esau, the innocent [afflicted] by the guilty, the just by
> the unjust. But yet, so far as he is able, he is at peace with
> everyone . . . .
>
> In a metalworker's workshop, a file is essential. [It is used]
> to scrape the rust from iron until it becomes gleaming and
> polished. The same is true of a wicked man who lives his
> life as part of a community. Even though he injures himself
> and seeks to injure others, those he persecutes he also "files"
> and purifies.[27]

And we mustn't forget that when it comes to communities,
they are not all monastic! Is there anyone who is not part of some
group and does not find there some human foibles?

Baldwin is not a dreamer or a utopian: he is a realistic person.
Reading his works, you notice that he must have had a violent
temper, leaning toward harboring grudges, and vindictive. Three
times he recognizes that it is not a small thing for him to have to
pardon some enemies and love them. He almost reproaches the
Lord Jesus for having made the yoke of the old Law heavier by
this precept that did not exist before. Previously it was legitimate
to hate your enemies; now, you must love them! But he triumphed
over himself. Later, he became bishop of Worcester, archbishop
of Canterbury, accompanied his king on the Crusade, and died
at Tyre. We should read with respect this witness of a life in
the bosom of a community (because he confides to us what he
practiced himself):

> A peaceable way of life in the midst of our brethren is,
> therefore, recommended for us, and although [such a life]
> may be less pleasant for the good [who dwell] among the
> wicked, it is often more useful. But for the good [who dwell]
> among the good, it is both useful and full of delight. There is

27. Baldwin, Tract 5; CF 39:140.

nothing in human life better than mutual love nor anything
sweeter than holy fellowship. To love and be loved is a
sweet exchange, the joy of one's whole life, the recompense
of blessedness. . . .

The unity of the religious life is a symbol and in some
ways an expression of that celestial fellowship in which,
through the communion of love, things which are particular
to each separate individual are found to be common to all.
Here indeed is the merit, but there is the reward; here is
the figure, there is the truth. Here our rest is begun, there
it is perfected. Perfect rest cannot be found in this place of
affliction, this place of pilgrimage. For us, the fullness of rest
is not to be found outside our inheritance.[28]

After denouncing the "triple unrest" which puts an obstacle
in the path of the desired rest, that is to say the malice of the world,
the malice of our own heart, and the malice, the wickedness of
others, Baldwin explains them and proposes a remedy for each
of them. We will not follow him in all those details, but we will
transcribe the personal prayer which he made to be freed from the
evil which came from himself, from his own concupiscence:

O Lord God, you alone are the repose of souls, and there
is no peace for us from all this misery save through you
and in you. As for me, [when I sought] to find rest in you,
I turned to your inheritance in which you are at rest, and
I said, "I shall abide in the inheritance of the Lord." This
I said with my mind's resolve, my heart's desire, and the
vow of my profession. Grant me now that I may say, "He
that made me rested in my tabernacle." Build in me your
tabernacle and rest in me, that I may rest in you. For this
is your rest: to effect our rest. Work therefore in me, that I
may love you before all things and above all things, that
I may desire nothing apart from you, nothing at all, save
only you or for your sake. Thus will I find peace, and in my
heart will be rest. . . .

What blessedness I could claim—or rather, [what
blessedness] I would feel in my heart—if I flamed with
desire for you alone and, burning and yearning, could with

28. Baldwin, Tract 5; CF 39:141–142.

the prophet say, "What have I in heaven, and what do I desire on earth but you?"[29]

Hasten to enter into that rest!

To the nuns whom he guided toward the summits of union with God, **Gilbert** addressed these words:

Hasten, consecrated virgin, hasten to enter into his retreat![30]

Well, what is that rest? That of the "little bed" [of the Song of Songs], that of the experience of union with the Bridegroom; an instant of such grace gives strength to endure a good many pains:

Let [the nun] experience what [she] is awaiting, "for good is the Lord" to those who wait for him, "to the soul which seeks him." This experience of an hour brings gladness to the labors of many seasons.[31]

The nun should not fear the drawn swords: they may correct others and stir them on; as for her, they will only wound her with love:

You they wound more gently, that transfixed by perfect love you may know nothing of alarms by night and may have no blend of chilling fear, but may pass wholly into the affection of burning love, for you have been consecrated to the undivided practice of love—*quæ in solum amoris es usum dicata*—.[32]

That holy rest so recommended by our Fathers is not laziness or unproductiveness. It is *otium*. Let me say again, that word has a positive value. It is its opposite, *negotium*, which is negative, which denies rest: business, "affairs," that is what is opposed

29. Ps 73. Baldwin, Tract 5; CF 39:146–147.
30. Gilbert, SC 16.9; CF 20:214. The French reads "d'entrer dans ce repos!", "to enter into that rest." That translation fits the development of the argument more clearly.
31. Gilbert, SC 16.8; CF 20:213. The English edition refers to a "brother" and "he."
32. Gilbert, SC 16.9; CF 20:214.

to holy rest. **William of Saint-Thierry** said admirably, and not without a certain indignation:

> Is leisure to devote one's time to God idleness? Rather it is the activity of all activities—*Otiosum est vacare Deo? Immo negotium negotiorum est!*—.[33]

The soul given up to God thinks of him, ceaselessly keeps [his] loving memory, which William again calls piety.[34] The Holy Spirit is pleased to come and rest on the humble and tranquil soul. It is the famous word that these old Cistercian authors read in their Bible, in the last chapter of Isaiah:

> On whom shall my spirit rest, if not on the humble, tranquil man who respects the Word of the Lord?
>
> The Holy Spirit can not come, **Bernard** says, except on a tranquil spirit; Christ does not come into a weak heart which vacillates.[35]

---

33. William, Ep frat I.21; CF 12:39.
34. William, Ep frat I.9; CF 12:18.
35. Bernard, V Nat 6–10.

IV   REST IN THE HEART OF CHRIST

We find among the Cistercian authors a fairly large number of texts on the wounds, and above all on the bosom of Jesus, on his open side. That wound in the side permits looking inside, as John invites us to do at the end of his Gospel. It is also an invitation to enter, to rest, or at least to take shelter.

Let's review the principal things they have to say. It seems to me there will be among them ample matter for meditation, for wonder, for embracing love.

Gilbert of Hoyland

In his *Twelfth Sermon on the Song*, in the first section he speaks of those who, in the Church, are required to fulfill the duty of contemplation. They ought not to be lazy about this office; they ought not allow themselves to become torpid during their free time.

In the second section, he recommends that contemplatives *hide themselves in the caves of Christ*. It is a beautiful passage. We must force ourselves to have the eyes of an eagle in order to *contemplate*, because where the body is, where Christ is, there the eagles ought to gather:

> You, too, be like the eagle and use sharp eyes!
> grow accustomed to spiritual contemplation,
> perch in the rocks and linger on sheer cliffs of flint,
> or rather enter the caverns
> of that unique rock which is Christ.

Here he has taken a text from Isaiah:

"Go into your rooms," as Isaiah says, "shut your doors, . . . hide
yourselves a little while until the wrath is past."[1]
Hide forever, adds Gilbert, that your delight may last forever!

He recommends then entering into that retreat which is the
open side of Christ, in order to rest in the contemplation of God.
It is a matter of thinking of nothing other than the holiness of
God, of his perfection, not of ours (we are right in the subject
of our retreat!). The text of Psalm 71 already quoted serves to
articulate the thought:

Be mindful "of his justice alone."

Gilbert then goes on; he refers at the same time to a phrase
which immediately precedes the psalm verse quoted:
Enter the chamber of peace, the mighty works of the Lord
and to a phrase from Psalm 122:

for peace exists in his might.

Enter the chamber of peace, the mighty works of the Lord,
for peace exists in his might.

Be mindful "of his justice alone,"
"for what do you have that you have not received"?

To live in the side of Christ, to hide yourself there and
contemplate. At the same time a rest and a regarding. It is what
Gilbert calls the *observatory*, the house where you observe, where
you contemplate: *habitatio speculationis*.
The rest of the sermon develops this double theme of rest
and regarding, and speaks of the rest involved in contemplation.
The Bride of the Song will rest and sleep, like Saint John, on the
breast of Jesus:

Then I shall rest and my sleep will be sweet.[2]
John slept, as it were, reclining upon the breast of Jesus,
where are stored

1. Is 26:20.
2. Prv 3:24.

"all the treasures of the wisdom and knowledge" of God.
There is the place of true repose,
the calm of understanding,
the sanctuary of piety, the chamber of delight.
Sleep here
that you may see what John saw,
the Word in the beginning,
the Word with God
and the Word who was God,
and may understand in Christ coeternity with the Father.

It is really a sleep: the reason doesn't budge; all that belongs to the human mode is still. It is good to let those human modes sleep in favor of the divine experience, which is the divine mode of seeing, of knowing, and of loving:

It is good then that you should fall asleep
and be lulled to forgetfulness of human feelings and affections,
that you be enabled to dream such dreams.[3]

A rest on the bosom of Jesus, who permits a gaze which is not of this world and which, through the humanity of Christ, goes until it reaches his divinity.

Guerric

He recommends that we take refuge in the wounds of Jesus and make our nest there. We find that elevation in the *Fourth Sermon for Palm Sunday*:

Blessed is he who, in order that I might be able to build a nest
in the clefts of the rock,
allowed his hands, feet and side to be pierced
and opened himself to me wholly
that I might enter "the place of his wonderful tent"[4]
and be protected in its recesses.[5]

3. Gilbert, SC 12.1; CF 14:150–152.
4. Ps 43.
5. Ps 31.

The rock is a convenient refuge for the badgers,[6]
but it is also a welcome dwelling-place for the doves.
These clefts, so many open wounds all over his body,
offer pardon to the guilty
and bestow grace on the just.
Indeed it is a safe dwelling-place, my brethren, and a tower
of strength
in the face of the enemy,
to linger in the wounds of Christ, the Lord,
by devout and constant meditation.
By faith in the Crucified and love of him
a man keeps his soul safe
from the heat of the flesh,
from the turmoil of the world,
from the attacks of the devil.

The wounds of Jesus are therefore the sources of pardon and graces, at the same time as being a secure refuge where we find shelter against all spiritual evils. To find this accommodation, it is only necessary to make yourself meditate at length with faith and love on the Passion, on the wounds of the Savior.

Guerric in his turn refers to a text of Isaiah. It is not the one that Gilbert chose, but he invites us again to hide ourselves in the cracks in the rock:

Go into the rock, then, man;
hide in the dug ground.[7]

which Guerric comments on:

Go into the rock, then, man; hide in the dug ground.
Make the Crucified your hiding-place.
He is the rock, he is the ground, he who is God and man.
He is the cleft rock, the dug ground,
for "they have dug my hands and my feet."[8]

6. Ps 104.
7. Is 2:10.
8. Ps 22.

Hide in the dug ground . . .
in the very hands that were cleft, in the side that was dug.
For what is the wound in Christ's side but a door in the side
of the Ark
for those who are to be saved from the flood. . . .
For in his loving kindness and his compassion he opened his side in
order that the blood of the wound might give you life,
the warmth of his body revive you,
the breath [o]f his heart flow into you
as if through a free and open passage.
There you will lie hidden in safety until wickedness passes by.[9]
There you will certainly not freeze, since in the bowels of Christ,
charity does not grow cold.
There you will abound in delights.
There you will overflow with joys.[10]

We should recognize that Guerric has described well, and surely completely experienced before, the advantages that one finds in nestling oneself in the wounds of Christ. Isaiah saw the hurricane of the divine wrath fall upon the Israelites; he sounded the alarm: hide yourself in the cracks of the cliff, wait until the cyclone has passed! Guerric understands well that one can fear the God of holiness, dread his judgment. Therefore, seeing the life-giving wounds of Jesus on the cross offering a refuge to the unfortunate, he gives this order: Flee! Flee God Jesus, but flee toward his humanity, bury yourself in the cracks in his body, those great holes of nails and lance. But that is not all: in entering into that refuge, you find yourself as well. No more fear, but peace. Therefore, why not sing? And the sermon continues on that new theme.

In the sixth sermon, Guerric dreams of the dove that makes her nest in the holes in the cliff. The one who is nestled in the wounds of Christ can coo like the dove of the Song. In practice, it is a matter of joyously singing the praises of the Lord: we

---

9. Ps 57.
10. Guerric, Palm 4.5; CF 32:77–78.

remember his Passion, we imitate it; we meditate on the wounds of Jesus. It is a sweet melody in the ears of the Savior.

Aelred

He also invites us to hide ourselves in the wounds of Jesus in a precious little work which he addresses to his sister,[11] in the form of a letter: *Rule of Life for a Recluse*. It is a means of entering profoundly into Christ, of nourishing ourselves, of becoming senseless and drunk:

> Then one of the soldiers opened his side with a lance
> and there came forth blood and water.
> Hasten, linger not, eat the honeycomb with your honey,
> drink your wine with your milk.
> The blood is changed into wine to gladden you,
> the water into milk to nourish you.
> From the rock streams have flowed for you,
> wounds have been made in his limbs,
> holes in the wall of his body,
> in which, like a dove, you may hide
> while you kiss them one by one.
> Your lips, stained with his blood,
> will become like a scarlet ribbon. . . .[12]

William of Saint-Thierry

In his book *On Contemplating God*, he ardently desires to enter, to penetrate the wound in the side of Jesus, to go as far as his heart, to have a profound contact with his divinity, there, in the very heart of Jesus:

> Like Thomas, that man of desires,
> I want to see and touch the whole of him
> and—what is more—to approach the most holy wound in his side,

11. So Fr Thomas. Scholars have debated at length whether Aelred indeed addressed his own sister.
12. Aelred, Inst incl; SCh 76:141; CF 2:90–91.

the portal of the ark that is there made,
and that not only to put my finger or my whole hand into it,
but wholly enter into Jesus' very heart,
into the holy of holies, the ark of the covenant,
the golden urn,
the soul of our humanity that holds within itself
the manna of the Godhead.[13]

In the course of his *Sixth Meditation*, William speaks of all the divine treasures which, until the Passion, were locked up within Jesus, and which the lance of the centurion caused to spring forth. Those treasures were enabled to flow by that opening, and we are enabled to enter in order to profit by them:

Those unsearchable riches of your glory, Lord,
were hidden in your secret place in heaven
until the soldier's spear opened the side
of your Son our Lord and Savior on the cross,
and from it flowed the mysteries of our redemption.
Now we may not only thrust our finger or our hand
into his side, like Thomas,
but through that open door may enter whole, O Jesus,
even into your heart, the sure seat of your mercy,
even into your holy soul
that is filled with the fullness of God,
full of grace and truth,
full of our salvation and our consolation.[14]

To enter into that side, to contemplate, see, covet, seize, and to be as it were electrified, with an irresistible desire to imitate Jesus, to follow him, the one who is the Way:

Open, O Lord, the ark-door of your side,
that all your own who shall be saved may enter in,
before this flood that overwhelms the earth.
Open to us your body's side,
that those who long to see the secrets of your Son may enter in,

13. William, Contemp 3; CF 3:38.
14. William, Med; CF 3:131.

and may receive the sacraments that flow therefrom,
even the price of their redemption.
Open the door of your heaven,
that your redeemed may see the good things of God
in the land of the living,
though they still labor in the land of the dying.
Let them see and long, and yearn and run;
for you have become the way by which they go,
the truth to which they go,
the life for which they go.[15]

In his *Eighth Meditation*, William speaks of waiting for God in the heart of Jesus. Once more, the heart is mentioned. This wait here stabilizes the soul, puts it in repose. The side of Jesus is a hiding place where one waits, peaceful, the end of all the evils which assail us here below:

Lord, whither do you draw those whom you thus embrace
and enfold,
save to your heart?
The manna of your Godhead, which you, O Jesus,
keep within the golden vessel
of your all-wise human soul,
is your sweet heart!
Blessed are they whom your embrace draws close to it.
Blessed the souls whom you have hidden in your heart,
that inmost hiding-place,
so that your arms overshadow them
from the disquieting of men
and they only hope in your covering and fostering wings.
Those who are hidden in your secret heart
are overshadowed by your mighty arms;
they sleep sweetly, and in the midst of the clergy
look forward joyfully,
for they share the merit of a good conscience
and the anticipation of your promised reward.

15. William, Med; CF 3:131–132.

They neither fail from faintheartedness,
nor murmur from impatience.[16]

Bernard

There is more than one text on the wounds opened in the side of Christ. Sometimes he meditates on the blood of our redemption which ran from those openings, on the water and the blood which sprang from the chest of Christ, pierced by the lance. He sees the *Springs of the Savior* in those blessed wounds. Thus the celebrated *First Sermon for Christmas* is also called *Springs of the Savior*. The Tiny One brings us immense riches, the price of our salvation. On the cross, the treasure will be spread out: the wounds in hands and feet, the opening of the side will permit the treasure to spread out. Taking a phrase from the psalm, Bernard does not recoil from that realistic image:

Then the sack having been torn,
all the money which it concealed is spread out
as the price of our redemption.[17]

We find the same idea in the *Ninety-sixth Sermon on Various Subjects*. The four streams of blood that ran from the hands and feet of the Savior make him think of the four rivers of the terrestrial Paradise: Christ is our true paradise. We lost the paradise that our first parents enjoyed before their sin; God has given us a better one, in giving us his Son. Already in his sermon for Christmas, Bernard had this memorable phrase:

We have in our possession a much better paradise than that
of our first parents, and that paradise is Christ our Lord.[18]

Beyond that, the saint sees above all in the wounds, openings where one can find a sheltered place in which to rest and contemplate. So the *Seventh Sermon on the Psalm "Qui habitat"*:

16. William, Med; CF 3:141.
17. Bernard, Nat 1.8.
18. Bernard, Nat 1.6.

he evokes the open side of the Savior, the right side, opened after death, and he gives this spontaneous exclamation:

> Ah! if I could be the dove
> that nests in the hole in the rock,
> the hole in his right side![19]

In the *Forty-fifth Sermon on the Song of Songs*, he suggests this thought: to make your nest, like the dove, in the hole in the rock, is to linger in contemplation of Christ, it is to live in his wounds. The loving gaze of contemplation that rests on the humanity, and particularly on the sufferings of Christ, is a true living in the Savior and in his wounds.

A relatively long passage in the *Sixty-first Sermon on the Song of Songs* is more beautiful than those we have presented up to this point. One could call it *Living in the Wounds of Christ*:

> The clefts of the rock [are] the wounds of Christ. . . .
> Within them "the sparrow finds a home,
> and the swallow a nest where she may lay her young";
> in them the dove finds safety
> and fearlessly watches the circling hawk.[20]

Saint Bernard borrows several phrases from Scripture which guide his thought and make it progress. In the three texts which he chose, the word "rock" is found; the translation is very literal:

- "He has made me climb in the rock"[21]
- "He has fixed my feet upon the rock"[22]
- "The wise man built his house upon the rock"[23]

Rock is solid! The man who has built his house on the rock fears neither the violence of winds, nor torrents of water. Three ideas to which Saint Bernard returns, as is his habit, to inculcate them well in his hearers or readers:

19. Bernard, QH 7.15.
20. Bernard, SC 61.3; CF 31:142.
21. Ps 27.
22. Ps 40.
23. Mt 7:24.

- Elevation above the earth
- A very secure shelter
- Feet firmly planted

To live in the wounds of Christ by loving meditation is to have one's heart lifted, its life in heaven, as Saint Paul puts it;[24] and from there it is solid, it is secure:

> The rock, with its durability and security, is in heaven.

Later, another Scripture text is brought in, and the thought rebounds; the text contains the word "rock": "The rock is a refuge for the swallows."[25] Thus speaks Bernard:

> And really where is there safe sure rest for the weak except in the Saviour's wounds? There the security of my dwelling depends on the greatness of his saving power. The world rages, the body oppresses, the devil lays his snares: I do not fall because I am founded on a rock.[26]

One last Scripture text is going to be expounded: "He was wounded for our sins."[27] It is the contemplation of the Savior's wounds which gives confidence in salvation:

> I have sinned gravely, my conscience is disturbed but not confounded, because I shall remember the wounds of the Lord. For "he was wounded for our transgressions." What sin is so deadly as not to be forgiven in the death of Christ? If therefore a medicine so powerful and efficacious finds entrance to my mind, no disease, however virulent, can frighten me.

In the fourth section of this sermon, the same theme is amplified: contemplation of the wounds of the Savior to find salvation. Saint Bernard assures us that from the moment in which one finds confidence, everything which we are lacking is given to us in Christ on the cross who saves us: it is as though

---

24. Phil 3:20.
25. Ps 104.
26. Bernard, SC 61.3; CF 31:142–143.
27. Is 53:5.

salvation sprang from his wounds. He puts himself on the spot and speaks in the first person:

> But as for me, whatever is lacking in my own resources I appropriate for myself from the heart of the Lord, which overflows with mercy. And there is no lack of clefts by which they are poured out.

Now we find again the theme already encountered in the sermon on the Springs of the Savior, the goods of redemption which flow from the wounds of Jesus:

> They pierced his hands and his feet, they gored his side with a lance, and through these fissures I can suck honey from the rock and oil from the flinty stone[28]—I can taste and see that the Lord is good. He was thinking thoughts of peace and I did not know it. "For who has known the mind of the Lord, or who has been his counsellor?"[29] But the nail that pierced him has become for me a key unlocking the sight of the Lord's will. Why should I not gaze through the cleft? The nail cries out, the wound cries out that God is truly in Christ, reconciling the world to himself.

This passage is very beautiful, and the Latin is almost music with its assonances. You notice the wordplay: *clavis* reserans, *clavus* penetrans.

Finally the tenderness of Jesus, and behind it that of the Father, breaks forth into full daylight. Saint Bernard says it with a great deal of force and sweetness:

> The secret of his heart is laid open through the clefts of his body; that mighty mystery of loving is laid open, laid open too the tender mercies of our God, in which the morning sun from on high has risen upon us. Surely his heart is laid open through his wounds! Where more clearly than in your wounds does the evidence shine that you, Lord, "are good and forgiving, abounding in steadfast love"?[30] No

28. Dt 32:13.
29. Is 40:13.
30. Ps 86.

one shows greater mercy than he who lays down his life
for those who are judged and condemned.[31]

Contemplation implies passing beyond self, which Bernard is
careful to remind us of fairly often, for example when he describes
the steps of spiritual ascent. At the last, it is contemplation, and
one passes from the love of self for God to the love of God because
he loves us, then to the love of God for himself, for what he is.[32]
Here is what he says about it in the fifth section:

> My merit therefore is the mercy of the Lord. Surely I am not
> devoid of merit as long as he is not [devoid] of mercy. And
> if the Lord abounds in mercy, I too must abound in merits.
> But what if I am aware of my many failings? Then where
> failings abounded, grace abounded all the more.[33] And if the
> mercies of the Lord are from eternity to eternity, I for my
> part will chant the mercies of the Lord forever.[34] But would
> this be my own righteousness? "Lord, I will be mindful of
> your righteousness only."[35]

Once again alluding to a Scripture text, Bernard tells God
that his cloak is large enough to hide his sins and the treasures
of the divine goodness, "and those treasures are hidden for me
in the holes in the rock."

In the sixth section the holy abbot promises to live, to make
his nest as Guerric also put it, within the wounds of the Savior,
to contemplate such sweet humanity, while waiting for the
contemplation in heaven of the face of God:

> I will go then to these storerooms so richly endowed; taking
> the prophet's advice[36] I shall leave the cities and dwell in the
> rock. I shall be as the dove nesting in the highest point of the
> cleft, so that like Moses in his cleft of the rock I may be able
> to see at least the back of the Lord as he passes by. . . . He

31. Bernard, SC 61.4; CF 31:144.
32. So Bernard, Div 3 and 8.
33. Rom 5:20.
34. Ps 89.
35. Ps 71. Bernard, SC 61.5; CF 31:144.
36. Jer 48:28.

is great in his kingdom, but so gentle on the cross. In this vision may he come to meet me, in the other may he fill me full. "In your presence," says the psalmist, "you shall fill me with joy." Each is a saving vision, each is amiable; but the one in greatness, the other in lowliness: the one in splendor, the other in pale shadow.[37]

That is what the spiritual masters of Cîteaux say about the wounds of Jesus, particularly the one in his side. They invite us to look, to hide ourselves, to feed, to rest, to sleep the sleep of contemplation, to go beyond ourselves in meditation on the Passion, to go until we reach the divinity of Christ, as far as the eternal love of God.

37. Bernard, SC 61.6; CF 31:145–146.

V   FROM MULTIPLICITY TO UNITY

Here is an important topic; in one sense it is the summit. We will find here a complete theology, and also very practical teaching on how to conduct ourselves.

Called to unity with God!

Our Fathers became enthusiastic and went into ecstasy before that unity toward which all our spiritual life tends. They sighed after that union, that unity, with "O's" of amazement. **Isaac**, who is the least emotional of them, expresses himself thus in his *Fifth Sermon for All Saints' Day*:

> "This, Father, is my desire, that as we are one,
>   these may be one in us."[1]
> How loving-kind the divine desire, worthy of God,
>   full of gracious charity, a truly valid assurance of Truth!
>   *O unum unum*—O one uniquely one!
>   *O unum prorsus necessarium*—O one absolutely necessary!

All practical life is engaged:

> It is a unity for whose sake all the pleasure of this world
>   [is] to be left behind, all bitterness withstood,
>   all vice avoided and virtue embraced.[2]

They support themselves particularly on two scriptural texts to praise the unity they covet so much:

---

1. Jn 17:21.
2. Isaac, OS 5; CF 11:43.

Unum *est necessarium . . . Martha, Martha, . . . circa*
   plurima.
Martha, Martha, you fret and worry about *many things.*
   One thing only is necessary.[3]
Unam *petii a Domino, hanc requiram.*
One thing have I asked of the Lord and that have I
   sought . . .[4]

Secondarily, they support themselves on other texts, for
example: (litt.) "A great number will live beyond (this time), and
knowledge will be manifold."[5] It is precisely that knowledge is
"manifold" or "multiple" (you need a great many things to learn a
science!); wisdom, on the contrary, is one: an intuitive knowledge,
quite simple. Very simple people, without instruction, can have
this wisdom of God.

Here there is a complete **theology**.

Monastic theology and this theme

Here is the outline of this monastic theology: it is not a matter
of a set of treatises, as in scholastic theology, but of an overall
view of the entire divine economy as it regards mankind:

God first. He is one and he is triune. We must note that
multiplicity is not opposed to unity here, but resolves itself in
unity.

He creates **man** in his image and likeness. There is also
in man who is clearly "one," something of "trinity": memory,
reason, will, and that all makes up only one soul.

The soul obviously does not stay inert. Normally, very
easily before the fall, man *remembers* God, *thinks* of him, *loves*
him. Everything is well ordered in him; the body and everything
that belongs to the domain of the senses is submitted to the soul
which is completely occupied with God. Everything rises toward
God, there is a great *unity* in that *complex* being.

William of Saint-Thierry, in his treatise *On the Nature and
Dignity of Love,* and occasionally in his *Commentary on the Song,* as

3. Lk 10:41–42.
4. Ps 27.
5. Dt 12:4.

well as in his *Meditations*, speaks of the first man, Adam, created to rise thus toward God, in a perfect harmony of all his being. Among the other Cistercian authors, Bernard, Guerric or Isaac, we find passages where it is a question of the first state of man.

The **fall** came. Man who had been created in the image of God was disfigured. With his memory, his intelligence, his will, he was in the image of the Trinity, at the same time one and three. Now the structure of the soul remains, but instead of remembering God, thinking of him, loving him, raising himself simply toward him during his earthly life, while awaiting the blessed life, everything is disorganized, broken. Instead of unity, there is division and dislocation.

Fortunately, God lifts up man. He is the **Incarnation-Redemption**. He who is the **Image** of the Father, the Son whose equality with God both angels and men had begrudged and whose unique resemblance [to the Father] they had desired iniquitously, became man to recover the only recoverable creature among the two who had fallen.

He became man, and he invites man to imitate him. Now there is no longer danger for man in imitating the Image of the Father; on the contrary it is his salvation. If man allows himself to be drawn by this incarnate God, who is all Lovableness, at the same time he finds again the image (once again it is the image of God), and the road to heaven.

In heaven, there is perfect union with God. It is the perfect resemblance and image, "we will be like him, because we will see him as he is."[6]

You could make a table with four columns and follow the history of man in his relations with God, and this would be true for each person. The four columns:

Salvation—Image—Love—Unity and Multiplicity

Salvation: creation—fall—ransom by the Incarnation—Redemption—heaven

Image: creation in the image of God—the image disfigured—the image which is partially restored—the perfect image in heaven

6. 1 Jn 3:2.

Love: love which rises easily toward God—which became perverted—which, drawn by the lovableness of God in Christ Jesus, climbs again towards its source, God—perfected in heaven

Unity in Eden—lost by sin: on the contrary **Multiplicity**, disharmony within man, with God, with others—Jesus leads back to unity; in following him, a man finds himself simple, unified in himself; united, one with God, with his brothers—perfect unity in heaven: no discord within nor with God or others.

Theological and practical teaching of the Cistercians on this topic

Our Fathers have a complete **theological teaching** on unity and multiplicity, and their entire **practical life** is engaged in it. We can see the following four points:

1) We are displaced by the first sin

2) God has reestablished us through Christ

3) Inevitably there is multiplicity which we must accept, and which is even helpful

4) It is a great art to keep your soul unified, to unify it even in the midst of this multiplicity.

1) We are displaced persons

This is because of the sin of Adam and our own personal sins. There is disorder in us, conflicts, concupiscence, bad tendencies which come to light daily, even in our interior acts. We could burst into tears about it sometimes. Who has not known certain moments, in prayer when you are very close to God, you are completely one with him, you want only what he wants, and you feel like crying to have to fall back into your own mediocrity, your own fickle thoughts? Who has not known those moments in which you intensely desire a perfect liberation? You say with the psalmist: "O Lord, deliver my soul!"[7] You ardently desire heaven where you will sin no more . . . .

7. Ps 116.

Baldwin, in his *Fourth Tractate*, wrote:

> By the sin of disobedience man began to be at odds both
> with God and with himself.[8]

In his *Tenth Tractate*, he speaks of the internal divisions of
man. It is a question of the sinner, the man separated from God
(but we all feel these divisions and suffer from them):

> By withdrawing from God, who is always one and the same,
> man is divided [from God] by the wrath of his countenance,
> but he is also divided within himself. He is not always one
> and the same to himself but is continually changing—
> now one thing and now another—[–*alius et alius*–] and he
> fulfills that which is written: "A fool is as changeable as
> the moon."[9]
>
> He differs and disagrees so much with himself and is so
> much in dissension and discord that far from being one
> single person to himself, it would be difficult to find two
> people who could be more contrary! He wants something
> and then does not want it, and the same person takes turns
> in hating and loving, doing something and deciding not to,
> approving something and then condemning it, searching
> for something and throwing it away, caring for something
> and then neglecting it. When he begins something, it often
> irks him to have begun it, and when he has finished it, he is
> sorry he did it. His wishes and desires, his endeavors and
> projects, his thoughts and affections and impulses, change
> in a multitude of ways as if they always displeased him, and
> by all these [changes] he himself is changed.

After having prolonged this description of the division
within the heart of the sinful man, Baldwin adds that the just
man also suffers interior divisions:

> But is it only the wicked who are thus divided? What of the
> soul of a just man who occupies himself with worldly things
> and busies himself with a whole multitude of concerns and

8. Baldwin, Tract 5; CF 39:114.
9. Si 27:12.

is therefore less mindful of God [than he should be]? Is he not also divided? Is it not said to Martha, "Martha, Martha, you are anxious and troubled about many things!"[10] What purpose was there in saying her name twice? Was it not enough to say "Martha" one single time without repeating it as "Martha, Martha!" Or does the repetition mean that Martha was divided? "Martha," he says the first time, and then again, "Martha." It is surely a divided Martha, an anxious Martha, a troubled Martha; anxious to make provision for the future, troubled in attending to present needs. You are anxious and troubled about many things.[11]

One could set alongside this a fair number of texts of the same type from our Cistercian authors: of the complaint of what they call *miseria*, all that misery which each man finds, first in himself, then around him.

Saint Bernard has a curious sermon, the *Forty-fifth on Various Subjects*, where he makes a complete table of the divine economy in its relations with man. It is really an archetype of this monastic theology. He says that the human soul was created in the image of God, memory, intelligence, will; it ought to find its happiness in living in the Trinity. On the contrary, it turned aside, it found unhappiness. Then it fell. Man preferred to fall "through the choice of his own will." At that point, everything was broken, was shattered in pieces (there is the multiplicity!): memory, intelligence, will, and each in three pieces.

The Holy Trinity has come to repair that fall and its breakings: the Father has sent his Son, who has given us faith (the work that you have to do is to believe in him whom God has sent, said Jesus[12]; the Holy Spirit has poured out charity in our hearts[13]; from these two virtues is born the hope of returning to the Father. And here is a magnificent little sentence, a pearl!

---

10. Lk 10:41.
11. Baldwin, Tract 10.4; CF 41:86–87.
12. Jn 6:29.
13. Rom 5:5.

> It is through that trinity (those three virtues) that, as though by
> a trident, the most blessed Trinity has led forth from the deep
> mud to the lost blessedness the changing and fallen trinity.[14]

The Lord Jesus rose to heaven on the day of the Ascension.
Bernard, in a sermon for that feast, could not stop himself from
pointing out the contrast between our earthly life, so much in the
grip of vanity and of all sorts of miseries, and life in heaven:

> As for us, we live in a country where malice abounds,
> where wisdom is rare, "because the body which is corrupt
> weighs down the soul, and that earthly dwelling beats
> down the sense by the multiplicity of cares which agitate
> it endlessly."[15] By "sense" is meant here, in my opinion,
> intelligence. In reality it is lowered when it is occupied
> with numerous objects, instead of drawing in upon the
> exclusive recollection of that city in which it will one day
> live. Intelligence so occupied is fatally abased and tugged
> in a thousand ways. By "soul," Scripture means here the
> affections which, in the corruption of the body, are prey to
> various passions, which one cannot completely tame, still
> less cure, so long as the will does not seek one single object,
> and does not tend toward that unity.[16]

Always that lost unity, that multiplicity which importunes
us, and against which we must struggle, in leading ourselves
toward unity, in forcing ourselves to think of nothing but God,
at the same time accomplishing the duties of our state in life, in
turning our affections toward one alone, that is God.

2) God has reestablished us through Christ

Here is a passage from **Aelred**'s *Mirror of Charity*, at the
same time both theologically and spiritually elevated and very
practical, which aims to better our everyday behavior. Aelred
shows our state of misery, the image of God in us brought low,
and the restoration by Jesus, through his cross, of our trinity-

14. Bernard, Div 45.4.
15. Ws 9:15.
16. Bernard, Asc 3.1.

image. We can already find our equilibrium again, fix ourselves in unity, find everything in that "unum," have our memory, our knowledge, and our love absorbed by Jesus crucified:

> Memory is restored by the text of sacred Scripture, understanding by the mystery of faith, and love by the daily increase of charity.
>
> The restoration of the image will be complete if no forgetfulness falsifies memory, if no error clouds our knowledge, and no self-centeredness claims our love. But where will that be and when? This peace, this tranquillity, this felicity may be hoped for in our fatherland, where there is no opportunity for forgetfulness among those living in eternity, nor any creeping in of error among those enjoying the truth, nor any impulse of self-centeredness among those absorbed in divine charity.

> O charity eternal and true—*o æterna et vera caritas!*
> O eternity true and beloved—*o vera et cara æternitas!*
> O Trinity, eternal, true, and beloved—*O æterna et vera et cara Trinitas!*

It is there, in God, in adhering to the divine Trinity that we find the one necessary thing, rest in the **One**.

> There, there is rest, there peace, there happy tranquillity! There is tranquil happiness, there happy and tranquil joyfulness.
>
> What are you doing, O human soul, what are you doing? Why are you seized by so many distractions? *One thing alone is necessary.* Why so many? Whatever you seek in the many exists in the one. If you long for excellence, knowledge, delight, abundance, all is there, there to perfection and nowhere else but there.

Here then is one of Aelred's goals:

> When shall I come and appear before your face?[17] Who will give me the wings of a dove that I may fly away and be at rest?[18] Meanwhile let my soul grow wings, Lord Jesus; I

17. Ps 42.
18. Ps 55.

ask, let my soul grow wings in the nest of your discipline.
Let it rest in the clefts of the rock, in the hollow of the wall.
Let my soul meanwhile embrace you crucified and take a
draught of your precious blood.[19]

Farther on, in the same *Mirror of Charity*, Aelred speaks of
three sabbaths: the *sabbath of days* (that of each week); the *sabbath
of years*: seven years, then a sabbatical year; seven weeks of years,
then a jubilee year, *sabbath of sabbaths*. That is the sign of unity.
Here is how Aelred goes into ecstasy before that unity, and
finds there an application in the unity which ought to reign in
a community:

> The sabbath of sabbaths . . . consists of seven sabbaths of
> years plus one, so that the number seven, which proceeds
> from unity and is perfected in unity, may be concluded in
> unity.
>
> Likewise, every good work is founded on faith in the
> one sole God and progresses by the seven-fold gift of the
> Holy Spirit to reach him who is truly one, where all that
> we are is made one with him. And because there is no
> division in unity, let there be no outpouring of the mind
> in various directions, but let it be one in the One, with the
> One, through the One, around the One, sensing the One,
> savoring the One—and because always one, always resting,
> and therefore observing a perpetual sabbath.[20]

Permit me to quote these last phrases in Latin to highlight
all these instances of *unum*.

> *Sit unum in uno, cum uno, in unum: unum sentiens, unum
> sapiens; et quia semper unum, semper requiescens, et sic perenne
> sabbatum sabbatizans!*

Do not think that we have here only a piece of fiction, a piece
of bravado: this was the life of those monks; it ought to be ours.
Seeking after God alone, the rest follows, but it becomes more
or less unimportant.

19. Aelred, Mir I.14–17; CF 17:94–96. Emphasis added by Fr Thomas.
20. Aelred, Mir III.1; CF 17:221.

3) Unavoidably there is some multiplicity which we must endure and which is even helpful

Abandon everything else? Yes and no . . . Obviously we must not let the other things dominate us, but the other things exist, and we cannot ignore them at our will. Father Eymard, recently canonized, said: "We must not let action rule us, we must rule it." We must take account also of the difference in graces and the difference in temperaments. There are many nuances; the Cistercian writers did not lack discretion.

The text which I will cite here from **Saint Bernard** is very practical, because he recommends union within the community, while respecting the diversity of the gifts of the Spirit; thus unity and pluralism. The text comes from the *Second Sermon for Septuagesima*. Bernard speaks of all the distraction that we experience here below: the things below us mire us down; we are not able to reach those that are above us. He quotes a phrase from Scripture which points out the unhappy state of man: "Unhappy man that I am! Who will deliver me?"[21] He recognizes that just one thing is necessary; nevertheless, down here action is necessary at the same time as contemplation, the single and the multiple, which he calls here unity and division:

> Nevertheless we must maintain unity and division at the same time. So it was that Adam slept in contemplation and afterwards named all the animals. So it was that the patriarch Abraham divided the animals in two, except the birds, in a sacrifice, and that Martha troubled herself with many things. Yes, there is only one thing necessary, just one thing absolutely necessary: it is the better part which will never be taken away.

Here below there will always be the two parts, contemplation and action. We have to adjust to that; only in heaven will this division cease.

> The division will cease when the fullness arrives, and when there is common participation in all the holy city of

21. Rom 7:24.

Jerusalem. But while we wait, the Spirit of wisdom is not only unified, it is also multiple: he consolidates the interior realities in unity, and distinguishes the exterior realities by judgment. We find the same phenomenon in the primitive Church; in effect, when "the multitude of the believers had but one heart and one soul," it was the birds which were not divided, and when "they distributed to each according to his needs," it was the animals which were cut in half.

Here is the practical application for the community of Clairvaux, which is true always and for all communities:

May there be also among us, my dearly beloved, unity of
    spirit. May our hearts be united
in loving one thing—*diligendo unum*
in seeking only one thing—*quærendo unum*
in adhering to only one thing—*adhærendo uni*
in feeling the same emotions—*idipsum invicem sentiendo.*

So much for the interior, for union and unity of souls; then without danger there could be diversity of exterior actions, according to the gifts of each person:

Here is how exterior divisions will be without danger and will not cause any scandal; each one will have his part to play, each one will have, in more than one case, his own manner of judging how to behave in worldly affairs; perhaps each will distinguish himself from the others by the different gifts of graces. One will not see all the members [of the community] given to the same actions; but the interior union and the harmony of feeling will make a single whole from the multiplicity, will draw them together by the glue of charity and the bond of peace.[22]

Isaac as we will recall[23] showed his admiration for unity in a very beautiful text:

O unique unity, O unity uniquely one, O absolutely necessary unity!

22. Bernard, Sept 2.3.
23. See the first pages of this chapter.

Immediately he adds something which was purposely kept until now:

> Unity toward which one runs *by a multiplicity of paths*, in which in simplicity, one stops, one rests, one takes delight.[24]

There is truly rest in unity, but we obtain it by multiplicity. Not everything about multiplicity is negative: if one handles it well, it leads to unity. We must often run about because of the activities which require our attention, which distract us, but we can greatly profit from that: we can transform them into unity, we can stop ourselves, and be at rest. We will see this more explicitly in the fourth point. But first, let us look at another of **Isaac**'s texts which will throw a great deal of light on this problem of unity and multiplicity, which is at the base of the action-contemplation problem, seen in a certain way. What marvelous equilibrium, what a healthy spirituality! It is taken from his *Twelfth Sermon*:

> This you see is the true norm of monastic life—
> to be in thought and desire at home
> in the everlasting fatherland with Christ,
> and yet shirk no kind service that can be done for Christ's sake
> during the toilsome journey through [t]his life;
> to be willing to follow Christ the Lord
> on his upward journey to the Father
> and thus become clear-sighted, purified and revived in medi[t]ation,
> not to refuse to follow Christ's going down to one's brother,
> and th[r]ough such activity being everywhere by turns to everyone,
> and
> being full of distractions and interruptions.
> Nothing that may be done for Christ's sake must be despised
> and nothing must be desired that is not for Christ's sake;
> Christ is ever the one and only source
> of that longing for him that finds expression
> both in the leisure that concerns itself with Christ as one,
> and in the willing service of many where Christ is manifold.[25]

24. Fr Thomas's interpretation. Cf. CF 11:43.
25. Isaac, 3 p Epi 12; CF 11:101.

That reminds me of what **William** said of Saint Paul:

> The charity of God lifted him on high, but charity for
> neighbor pressed him down like a weight hanging from
> his neck.[26]

*4) It takes great skill to know how to keep your soul one, even to unify
it, in the middle of all this multiplicity*

One thing is certain: the saints arrive at a great unity in
their interior life. They can be more or less given over to exterior
activities: they have an internal life which unifies everything,
allowing them to assimilate everything and to rest united with
God in all their labors.

One other thing is certain: you notice in every spiritual life,
to the degree that it is advancing, a simplification comes into
play, which grace effects which allows the person to give himself
over to many activities, to take part in all sorts of situations,
while keeping and displaying a growing and profound unity
which makes us think of the divine unchangeability: progress
in simplicity, progress in internal peace, progress in the peace
which without our realizing it shines out; those who have arrived
at this stage are *peace-full people*. They make peace and spread it
around.

At bottom it is this serenity, considered by our Fathers as
the pinnacle of the spiritual life, the imperturbability, without the
least pride, of those old monks and nuns, and perhaps of those
old mothers, whom we all know who are or who were "nothing
but prayer." They had almost nothing but God, and God was
enough for them; he filled their lives.

In the midst of a crowd, Saint Bernard could make for
himself solitude in his heart and pray as if he were alone.[27] From

---

26. William, Nat am 22; CF 30:79.
27. William, Vita Bern; *Vita Prima*, 32.

the time of his novitiate, he could give himself completely to his exterior manual labor, and keep all his interior union with God. Brother Laurence of the Resurrection, that seventeenth-century Carmelite who had such an experience of the presence of God, recognized that in the kitchen attacked from several sides at once, and flipping his omelet at the same time, he was as united to God as he was when praying before the Holy Sacrament.

Normally the Spirit of God pushes us to become more simple, to the degree that we are advancing in the spiritual life, to become more one within, to pass from multiplicity to unity.

In his *Counsels to Novices*, **Meister Eckhart** said this:

> The person who is at his ease, is at his ease in all places and among all people. The person who is not at his ease is not at his ease in any place or with anybody. But he who is at his ease truly has God near him. Then he who has God honestly and truly near him has him in all places, both in the street and among the whole world, as well as in the churches or in solitude or in his cell. If he always has him honestly, and if he has him all the time, no one can get in his way.
>
> Why? Because he has only God and thinks only of God and that all things come to him only from God. The person carries God in all places and in all his works, and it is only God who performs all the works of that person. Because the work belongs more appropriately and truly to the one who causes the work than to the one who performs it. If then we have nothing in our thoughts but God, and him alone, in truth he ought to perform our work, and in all his works, nothing can block him, neither the crowd nor places. So no one can block that man, because he thinks of nothing but God, he seeks nothing but God, he enjoys nothing but God: because God unites himself to that man in all his aspirations. And just as no multiplicity can distract God, neither can anything distract or scatter that man any more, because he is in the One, where all multiplicity is unity and a non-multiplicity.[28]

28. Cited in *Vie spirituelle* (1982) 216–217.

Baldwin has a page in his *Sixth Tractate, On the Power of the Word of God*, on the mishmash of the feelings, of the affections of the soul, when it addresses itself to God, and how nevertheless charity gathers all that together into a unity which resembles the unity of God:

> God is spirit,[29] and he who cleaves to God is one spirit [with him].[30] But since the human spirit is totally divided and dispersed within itself, it can only be collected together and united by joining itself to God, who is one and simple. Yet even when it joins itself to God, it divides itself up, for in seeking to join itself to him and be joined to him more closely, it joins itself to him in a whole variety of different ways. But who is capable [of enumerating these]? Who can count every single rapturous outpouring of awe, wonder, amazement, meditation, or contemplation? Who can count all the pricks of his conscience, the joys of devotion, the bursts of rejoicing, the extent of his yearning, his sobs and his sighs, his burning desires, and earnest prayers? Only he who counts the days of the world and the drops of rain, he alone, can comprehend and count them! The mind which is fixed in the love of God is subject to countless loving passions and is drawn [to God] in countless ways; but although its affections interchange and alternate in a marvelous manner, its love still remains constant and immovable. When it changes within itself in so many different ways, it is certainly divided [in its approach] *to* God, but it is not divided *from* God.[31]

It is in effect love that creates unity. **William of Saint-Thierry** had good reason to write in his *Commentary on the Song*:

> She who loves but one person is unmoved and wanders not.[32]

---

29. Jn 4:24.
30. 1 Cor 6:17.
31. Baldwin, Tract 6; CF 39:166–167.
32. William, Cant 4.60; CF 6, 48.

It is love that creates unity: it has a force, a cohesive energy. Without wanting to engage ourselves in too much speculation, let us think again of those old holy people, of those old monks and those old nuns who are sometimes quite ill, but whose souls have been pacified, marvelously serene. God is their great good, they think of him almost always, they love him. They are in their place before him, that is to say, humiliated, humble. They do not prefer themselves to others, rather they consider others better than themselves, they think well of others. At the root of this whole attitude of truth, there is charity: they love, they are united within themselves, united to God, united to their brothers and sisters.

A holy self-mocking saying (remember the prayer of Mgr Saudreau . . .) is to say to yourself: "There is nothing but God, what does the rest matter to us?"

VI PASSING FROM THE OLD MAN TO THE NEW

If we speak of the "old man," obviously it's not in order to make him look good, to flatter him, to spare him, but to be pitiless toward him, to mistreat him, to make him die. But I believe that our threats, our declarations of war, our decisions to execute him once and for all must not make much impression on him, because after we act like that, he knows what to hang on to, he knows that at bottom we treat him, if not like a good friend, at least not like an enemy, anathematized, with whom we do not by any means want to make a treaty.

Our old man, we groan about him, we wish him dead, but at the same time we love him well . . .

We must strip ourselves of him nevertheless, because he cannot enter into heaven with us. Then why put it off until later, until the last moment? We must, with the help of grace, have a firm will to aim for perfection, therefore to get rid of everything which is defective and makes us fall into sin. It takes a lifetime.

Saint Bernard used to say to postulants who were in a hurry to enter: "If you're in such a hurry for what is inside . . . "; we have already encountered this phrase. Now it is necessary to say what he added:

> If you're in such a hurry for what is inside, then abandon here on the outside those worldly bodies of yours. Here only spirits should tread; the flesh profits nothing.[1]

Because the future novices were terrified by such words, with greater mercy he explained to them that it was the concupiscence of the flesh, which it was necessary to leave outside.

1. William, Vita Bern; *Vita Prima*, 27.

It's easy to say leave concupiscence, in other words the old man, at the door! In practice, as in all times, he came in. Undoubtedly, he kept himself quiet the first few weeks, then he reappeared, and it was necessary to struggle hard.

To struggle energetically, counting above all on grace, yes that falls well within the scope of this retreat: to go beyond yourself, to pass from self to God.

Bernard, from the time of his entry at Cîteaux, struggled thus with all his ardor:

> He . . . insisted on mortifying, not only the concupiscences of the flesh, as actualized through the bodily sense, but even the very senses through which the actualizing occurred [sic].[2]

Here is what **William** notes again about his hero to point out the severe control exercised over the senses:

> He aimed to allow [the senses] just enough scope to maintain association and outward dealings with other people.

That became a habit, which itself became second nature.

On the other hand, *an interior sense* was born and developed. It was to protect it that Bernard reined in so hard the use of the exterior senses. It is *the sense of illuminated love*. Here is what it is in the vocabulary of William himself.

What did **William** mean by this sense of illuminated love? It concerns a special action of the Holy Spirit who seizes the person's heart and loves it in a divine way. It is a very strong *impression*, a sort of wound. The heart is "affected." This happens particularly when the person is in the midst of loving, for example while considering the Passion of our Lord, as William does in his *Tenth Meditation*. Suddenly one is seized in the face of so much of God's love. Seized, impressed, affected, it is the same phenomenon. The soul so touched undergoes a blessed *transformation*, it is changed. Into what? Into what she feels, *into that goodness of God*. I believe that we can very well conceive what that means, and that each of us has only to go back to his own experience: those moments of

2. William, Vita Bern; *Vita Prima*, 27–28.

prayer, when one is seized by that excessive, crazy love of God, and we stay completely bound up in it. We think then, perhaps without formulating it too much, like **Saint Bernard**:

> How wonderful your love for me, my God, my love!
> How wonderful your love for me . . . .[3]

We feel everything has changed at that moment, deriving a new goodness from the goodness of God. And isn't it true that this gives us a new knowledge of God, God who is essentially Goodness, Love? Yes, and William insisted in an extraordinary manner on that knowledge which is a superior understanding, not based on reasoning, but on experience—experience of love, *illuminated love*. Since it is an experience, we cannot help comparing it to the experience, which our senses give us. When God, when the Holy Spirit acts this way in us, let us say "acts on us," in a certain way we see, we hear, we taste, we touch, we feel. It is a superior understanding by means of illuminated love. Like all knowledge (William explains in three places, above all in his *Third Meditation*), it is the basis of transformation into what we know: God impresses, prints in the depth of the soul something of what he is; we become slightly divinized.

Well, that is what **Bernard** began to experience, from the time of his novitiate. He gave himself to a somewhat ferocious recollection, but he felt that to be necessary to become open to the work of the Holy Spirit in his soul. He reserved himself for God. He confides in us in his *Forty-third Sermon on the Song*: from the time of his entry at Cîteaux, from his "conversion," he applied himself to thinking assiduously on the Passion of his Lord Jesus, to keeping a constant remembrance of it. He united like a bouquet all the sufferings of his Master; that absorbed him. There precisely is a phrase, which William employs to characterize Bernard's behavior during his novitiate:

> His whole self became absorbed in the spirit, his whole hope steered towards God . . . seeing he did not see, hearing he did not hear.[4]

3. Bernard, SC 17.7; CF 4:131.
4. William, Vita Bern, 20; *Vita Prima*, 28.

This transformation in the times of strong union with God marked him deeply. The divine image was remade in him; he became more and more the *new man*, a new creature, and the *old man* died in him.

We have not wasted our time considering what happened in concrete detail, lived by a man, by Saint Bernard, from the beginning of his monastic life. Now, let's look at things in a more didactic way, while still very practical, formulating two points which will be developed with supporting texts: the Cistercian authors speak of the old man in a *theological* way and in a *practical* way, to help their brothers struggle generously against the old man.

1) Theological point of view

Man was created beautiful, good, in the image of God, all set to raise himself toward God. No internal struggles, everything was perfectly ordered. Man *remembered* God, he *thought* of him, he *loved* him. It's precisely in being completely occupied with God with his entire soul, memory, intelligence and will, that he was a beautiful image of God, a shining image: the Trinity *shone* in him, according to a phrase of **William of Saint-Thierry**.[5]

Sin has dislocated everything, cast it down; the divine image has been soiled and disfigured.

For **Bernard**, the first step towards sin, the first deviation, was Eve's *curiosity*. She looked at the fruit. Her soul, instead of keeping watch over itself, gave way to curiosity which was the occasion and cause of the sin which was to be committed. Curiosity is contrary to "being with self" (recollection) as well as to "being with God." The recollection, "being with self" is termed unity; curiosity, "going out of self" is called dispersion or multiplicity. This tirade against curiosity is found in the treatise *The Steps of Humility and Pride*.[6]

Adam fell. He was robbed and wounded, like the man of the parable on the road to Jericho. So **Aelred** described him, in

---

5. William, Nat am 3.24,25; CF 30:54.
6. Bernard, Hum 30; CF 13A:58–59.

a sermon for Ascension. Here is Adam, and all men with him, with the wounds of error, of shameful passions, of anger, of hate . . . :

> O unhappy Adam, what do you have to do with Jericho? Jericho means "moon." Therefore "the insensitive person changes like the moon."[7] You have descended, poor unfortunate one, you have changed, passing from charity to cupidity, from truth to blindness of spirit, from eternity to death.
>
> We could well say that you have fallen into the hands of brigands: ignorance is a brigand, concupiscence is a brigand, anger is a brigand. These brigands rob you, O unfortunate one. Ignorance robs the soul of wisdom, concupiscence robs the flesh of its purity, anger robs the spirit of its tranquility. They also inflict wounds: ignorance the wound of error, concupiscence that of the passions, and anger those of hate and acrimony. In the whole universe, this unfortunate Adam goes around half dead: dead in the majority of his descendants, he is alive only in a few good people by faith and works.

Then **Aelred** shows that the good Samaritan, Christ, has come "without having taken the same road . . . : he has certainly come of Adam's flesh, but not from Adam's sin."[8]

We are also, for **Bernard**, the wounded man of Jericho; he says it in his *Sixth Sermon for Christmas Eve.*[9] It is a good thing that Christ has come, because otherwise we would be:

lost   **unhappy**   **hopeless**

He bears three names (stated during the formal announcement made in the chapter room by the cantor, at which all prostrate themselves):

Jesus   **Christ**   **Son of God**

born today in Bethlehem of Judea.

---

7. Si 27:12.
8. Aelred, SI 13; PdC 27:63–65.
9. Bernard, V Nat 6.1.

Jesus, Savior, what more is necessary for the lost?
Christ, what more wanted, more desirable for the unhappy?
Son of God, what more useful to the hopeless?

Bernard invites us to *ruminate*, to exult in ruminating on and "bringing up" this good word.

Elsewhere, the same **Bernard** says that evil invaded, occupied our hands, our mouth, our heart;[10] or again, in another sermon, evil invaded our heart, our mouth, our body:[11] it was "the earthly man." The entire sermon is about interior renewal. Heart, mouth, body, all was made old in us, and all is renewed by the Lord Jesus. He lives in the heart as Wisdom Christ, in the mouth as Truth Christ, in the body as Justice (Holiness) Christ. One could easily make up a table so well does Bernard expose his ideas, classifying, dividing, and summarizing them. For each of the elements, heart, mouth, and body, he takes note of the factors of aging and the renewal due to Christ.

Baldwin wrote a whole tractate on the *necessity of crucifying the old man* (the Eleventh, which was supposed to be the first in the original collection). It is worth reading and meditating on. Taking expressions from Saint Paul, he speaks successively of the *earthly man*, the *fleshly man* (*carnalis*), and of the *animal man*. The earthly man is the ordinary man, the one in us that wants earthly things. The carnal man is the man submitted or sold to sin; he feels concupiscence and consents to it. The animal man, the "psychological" man as Paul put it, is the man riveted to nature, "natural" in the lowest sense of the word.[12]

Christ came; he was the good Samaritan. He is really the savior, and merely pronouncing his name heals and saves, says **Bernard**, in a very beautiful sermon on the Song, in the place where he comments on the phrase: "Your name is [perfumed] oil poured out."[13]

These hands, this mouth, this heart in which the old man resided—now Christ is the one who lives there. **Bernard** says

10. Bernard, Adv 5.3.
11. Bernard, Div 69.
12. Baldwin, Tract 11; CF 41:94 ff.
13. Bernard, SC 15.6–7; CF 4:109–111.

it with realistic details in his *Fifth Sermon for Advent*, following what was quoted above:

> Now if a new creation is accomplished in him, the past is destroyed; in place of crime and shame, man carries in his hands innocence and chastity. In his mouth, instead of arrogance and detraction, the humble vow and the word which edifies. In his heart, charity and humility have taken the place of carnal pleasures and temporal glory.[14]

All this is bound up with the *theme of the image*: we used to bear the image of the first Adam; now we bear that of the second Adam, even though we are not completely quit of the old man.

In a sermon for Christmas, **Bernard** says again that man was made in the image of God. A deceiver came; he promised a new seal, but he broke the seal of the divine image. After the coming of Christ, the Image of the Father, came the renewal.[15]

The *Tenth Tractate* of **Baldwin**, *On the Seal of the Love of God*, should be read here. Man has been marked that way on the day of his creation and on that of his redemption:

> In loving us and wanting to be loved, God fashioned a seal, and upon it was engraved the image of love. With this he sealed our heart clearly and firmly so that it received in itself a likeness of his image which was patterned on his image, a likeness which expressed his image by showing forth the same figure.
>
> [By the word] "seal" you must understand on the one hand the one who does the sealing and on the other the one who is sealed . . . . Christ, however, both seals and is sealed, for on him has God the Father set his seal. . . . Through him, God has sealed us, as it is written, "We have been sealed, O Lord, with the light of your countenance." He sealed us on the day of our creation when he formed us in his image and likeness. He sealed us on the day of our redemption when he re-formed us according to his image.[16]

---

14. Bernard, Adv 5.3.
15. Bernard, Nat 2.3.
16. Baldwin, Tract 10; CF 41:74–75.

2) Practical point of view

Sorting through the texts where our Fathers speak of the old man, it seems we can group what they say around these two ideas: *acknowledgement that the old man lives in us* and *what we ought to do about it.*

The old man lives in us

They note that the old man still lives in them, that he is lively, and that they must struggle energetically against him.

The *Twenty-seventh Sermon* of **Isaac of Stella** is a marvel. This abbot, one Quinquagesima Sunday, commented on the word of Christ: "Here we are going up to Jerusalem, and the Son of Man will be delivered to the Gentiles."[17] He confronts those religious with their vocation, with the exigencies, which it carries with it: a rigorous separation from the world, a generous effort to mount up and live in the spirit, from this life to heaven. It is necessary to disengage from everything to leap more easily, like the birds or other beasts that gather themselves together to spring or bound a great distance:

> Birds, in order to take their flight through the air, gather themselves as much as they can on the earth, pulling together their whole bodies. In the same way we, loving heaven, have separated ourselves from the world of men; hungry for fullness, we have thrown riches far from us; desiring honors, we have become like the refuse of this world![18] . . Let us draw back like rams [before they charge] to launch ourselves better toward that which is before us!

Basically, such texts are useful for all disciples of Christ. If all are not called to reject their riches, neither should they become attached to them. One should reread, above all on a retreat, what Jesus said about riches: "How difficult it is for a rich man to enter the Kingdom of heaven!"[19] Only the grace of

17. Lk 18:31.
18. 1 Cor 4:13.
19. Mt 19:23.

God can accomplish the miracle of having a heart detached from riches, while possessing them. "For men, it is impossible; but to God, all things are possible."[20] That is why Isaac continues, still addressing himself to his monks, but to all of us as well:

> Certainly, brothers, the summit we must climb is steep, the canyon which we want to file through is narrow! We must therefore be lightly equipped and slender. It is very difficult to climb with a bundle on your shoulders, or to glide through a narrow passage if you are corpulent. Not to be inflated by riches, nor bowed down by worries, nor made heavy by the excesses of the table takes a divine miracle: it is absolutely impossible to human weakness, but for God everything is possible.[21]

Isaac is going to face the old man now, to handle him roughly, to struggle with him without giving any quarter:

> Here is the rest of the text: "And the Son of Man will be given up to the Gentiles to be scoffed at and crucified."[22] Our old man, son of the old man [Adam] was crucified one day with the New Man, the Son of Man, according to the words of the Apostle: "Our old man has been crucified with Him."[23] That is why he must still be crucified within each of us, for as long as our [Good] Friday lasts.

Our author now expresses himself in the first person, but each of us is invited to make these words his own:

> No matter how much I seem in effect in my body and my soul, to be one person, I nevertheless find two in myself, and the sons of two men, the old man and the new, the earthly and the celestial, the son of man and the son of God.

In each of us the son of man struggles against the son of God trying to draw him to himself, to charm him; basically he hates him. The son of God in us struggles for his part against the son

20. Mt 19:23.
21. Isaac, PL 194:1778A–C; cf. SCh 207.141–143; translations differ.
22. Lk 18:32–33.
23. Rom 6:8.

of man, showing himself relentless against him; basically it is a true love:

> Thus the flesh fights and covets against the spirit, not in pushing it far from her, but more in drawing it to herself by caresses: "Each one," says the apostle James,[24] "is drawn by the attraction and the deceitful charm of his own covetousness." These are the hypocritical kisses of an enemy, even more dangerous than the blows or the reproaches of a friend. The son of man hates in me the son of God and persecutes him. The flesh seeks the spirit with its caresses and its murderous charms.
>
> On the contrary the son of God which I am, the new man who dwells within the old man, loves the one he fights, that son of man whom he strikes in order to make him better, whom he whips so that he will amend himself.[25]

We could have lengthened the quotation for some time, but let us be content with the conclusion, which strikes like the blow of a whip:

> Show yourselves now, my well beloved, cruel and hard against yourselves.[26]

In the *Twenty-ninth Sermon*, **Isaac** returns to the same subject: the son of God in us must govern the son of man; we will say no more about it here.

Aelred, in his *First Sermon on the Prophecies against the Nations*—or the "burdens," the Hebrew word was chosen because it had both senses—, said that Jesus raises his cross over the swells of our passions, calming them.[27] Elsewhere, in his *First Unedited Sermon*, he tells his brothers not to be astonished if the Lord arms himself with a pickaxe (*dolabrum*) to flatten our lumps![28]

In short, the old man is dead . . . and he is not dead, we must simply recognize it. **William**, in his *Exposition on the Epistle to the*

24. Jas 1:14.
25. Isaac, PL 194:1779C–1780A; SCh 147–149; translations differ.
26. Isaac, PL 194:1780C.
27. Aelred, Oner 1.3; PL 184:819C.
28. Aelred, SI 32.

Romans, says that the passions ruled before the coming of grace through faith; now they are not dead, but they no longer rule.[29]

We enjoined the postulant who presented himself to enter the monastery to leave his "old man" at the door; it is evident that he came in all the same! But it will be necessary to show yourself determined to kill him off.

Adam of Perseigne, who seems to have been novice-master at Pontigny, having become abbot of Perseigne, wrote a letter to Osmond, a monk of Mortemer, about the formation of novices, and he ends it:

> Greet your novices in my name, and on my behalf advise them so to direct their minds to a holy novitiate that with heart and soul they may renounce the worldly past [Père Robert translates: put on the new man].[30]

In another letter, addressed this time to a monk of Pontigny, he speaks again of novices and of the old man whom they ought to strip off; "novice" (new) is set in contrast to old, aged, obsolete.

> The novice worth the name strips off the ugliness of the old man, precisely in applying himself to a more rigorous life, which transforms him and gives him the beauty of the new man.[31]

In this same letter to G., monk of Pontigny, Adam talks about the newness which ought to characterize the novice, describing with a great deal of detail and precision four aspects of the "obsolescence" which the one who wants to give himself to God ought to reject, which therefore he ought to struggle against energetically. Every layperson that seeks intimacy with God will profit from this account:

> There are four main aspects under which this obsolescence presents itself to our view: love of the world, excessive concern for the body, a life of sin, and defense of the sin.

29. William, Exp Rm; PL 180:613B–C; CF 27:140.

30. Adam, Ep 5.64; CF 21:110.

31. Ep 11; PL 211:614C; Bouvet, *Archives du Maine Lettres d'Adam de Perseigne*, 504 (Let. 50).

Love of the world has three ways of ruining the soul by its oldness: it inflames the soul with the desire for honors, puffs it up with appetite for vain praise, burdens it to the point of crushing it under the weight of riches which it covets. All these evils either proceed from interior pride, or they supply it and bring food for it. For being inexorably infected with the poison of pride is to become aged and inevitably to decay, and then to be within two fingers' breadth of death.[32]

For Adam, all that was only a first step which led the young man who wanted to become a monk to the door of the monastery; the second aspect of oldness of which he must rid himself, *excessive concern for his body*, will mark his true entry:

He who in the first blush of his conversion has despised the world and so taken the first step towards his renewal, will take the second in entering the monastery, that is to say in relegating to second place the care for his own flesh, a care which nevertheless to take the Apostle's word for it, ought to be assured as far as necessary things are concerned, without yielding to covetousness.

It is necessary to take care of yourself to the point of nature, not of sin; it is necessary to pay attention to necessity and not yield to voluptuousness. God created our nature, but he is not responsible for sin. Neither should we hate or persecute that which does not resist its Creator; we ought to take care of our natural body and consecrate it to the service of its author; nonetheless, let us make war on the corruption and vices which do not come from God.

Adam then gives some wise precepts, insisting not on exterior practice but on interior disposition. In practice, we must follow the observances (let's say the commandments) but watch for interior fidelity above all, for the Holy Spirit:

Stable in faith, sociable in charity, frugal in way of life, what then dwells within this man that could prevent his soul from being attentive exclusively to the Holy Spirit?[33]

32. Adam, Ep 50; Bouvet, 505.
33. Adam, Ep 50; Bouvet, 508–509.

The third element of oldness, which Adam considers concerning the novice who has entered the monastery, is the *habit of sin*. He is the first one to be astonished that such an evil could exist in a man who has renounced everything to enter the cloister. The problem is that if, after having been converted [in the monastic sense] and purified, this man willingly abandons himself successively to thoughts of pride, then to dreams of advancement, if he is empty now of spiritual desires through his own fault, then he lets himself be invaded by the spirit of evil, and he falls or falls back into the habit of sin:

> But, you may say, how can a man who has already left the world and the flesh have the habit of sin? Nevertheless yes, he who has despised the world, shamed the flesh, renounced the pleasures of the flesh, finds himself still obliged to a continual combat against spiritual powers. Oh! How many men live today under the religious habit who apparently, escaping from the slavery of the devil and the flesh, have returned nevertheless in their hearts to Egypt and within themselves have fallen back into sin! Yes, their exterior conduct announces sanctity, they are vowed to it by the oath of their profession, but, with the name of the living, within they are dead since under the exterior appearance of poverty and continence, their spirit aspires nonetheless to the glory of an ephemeral praise or to the elevation to some dignity or other.

In the lines that follow, you can see the insistence on the action of the Holy Spirit: this man was formerly guided by him; now he has left him because of his fault, he has even chased him away:

> O what an exchange, and how unfortunate! He who had expelled from his spirit this world with its unclean prince, and had submitted his own spirit to the direction of the Holy Spirit, in vowing himself to live with him, chases him once more from himself, and places his spirit again under the reign of an unclean usurper! From that time on the hypocrite persecutes the Holy Spirit and puts him to flight, while, for his part, "the Holy Spirit of discipline flees the lie."[34]

34. Ws 1:5. Adam, Ep 50; Bouvet, 510–511.

The novice must fight against and avoid such an evil by fear and vigilance. It is not a matter of a servile fear: it is more the fear of one's self, the defiance of self, which **Saint Bernard** recommends so strongly in his *Fifty-fourth Sermon on the Song*.[35]

The fourth evil of oldness is the one **Adam** calls *the defense of the sin*. It is the annoying habit, which we have inherited from our first father, of always finding an excuse for our daily faults, or at least to have that tendency. Upon finding this evil, the abbot of Perseigne recommends avowing it in sacramental confession:

> It is necessary without ceasing and with constancy to confess these small things which are found in great abundance in the muck at the bottom of the heart, and which one ought to accuse and cry for before the priest.[36]

And Adam enumerates all these miseries which it is necessary to recognize in one's self:

> How often our soul lends an ear to the suggestions of the enemy! How often we run back complacently to the amusements of the world! How often, at divine office, we find ourselves somnolent and lukewarm! How often lazy and slow to obey! How often we neglect the need of our neighbor! How often we do to him what we would not want to suffer from him! How often we demand rigorously from him that which we would not be willing to do for him if he demanded it of us! Often we allow ourselves to be beaten down by adversity, often to be elated by success! Often in the good that the grace of God gives us or makes us accomplish, we seek not the glory of God, but our own glory! Often we dissimulate about what we ardently desire; often we put on an appearance of being other than that which we are . . . .[37]

The enumeration continues; that which has been quoted is enough to provide material for an examination of conscience for those who find nothing to accuse themselves of in confession!

35. Bernard, SC 54.10–12; CF 31:79–81.
36. Adam, Ep 50; Bouvet, 516.
37. Adam, Ep 50; Bouvet, 517.

You will note in that enumeration a great care for a strict purity of intention.

Little by little the beginner who has given himself to ascesis and the practice of virtues begins to renew himself, to clothe himself with the new man, as **William of Saint-Thierry** remarks in his book *The Nature and Dignity of Love*, in speaking of a young monk who has applied himself to follow the Rule, to submit himself to the discipline of the monastery, to take control of the old man:

> By all this, things begin to take on a new countenance for him. The better charisms [those which Saint Paul enumerates[38] where one finds the praise of charity], which he has labored until now to emulate, themselves begin to appear to him in a more familiar way. The body, humbled by holy discipline, begins to pass from habit, however good, to the spontaneous service of the spirit. The inner countenance of the new man begins to be renewed day by day until it is unveiled to behold the good things of God.[39]

Saint Bernard, in his *Sixty-third Sermon on the Song*, observes with joy the progress, which manifests itself even in the exterior comportment of the novices at Clairvaux:

> Do you see these novices? They came recently, they were converted recently. We cannot say of them that "our vineyard has flowered": it is flowering. What you see appear in them at the moment is the blossom; the time of fruiting has not yet come. Their new way of life, their recent adoption of a better life—these are blossoms.[40]

What we must do

Evidently it is necessary to struggle against the old man: a generous effort is required; only those who struggle violently ravish heaven, but above all grace is necessary, and only God can give it.

---

38. 1 Cor 12:31.
39. William, Nat am 10; CF 30:63.
40. Bernard, SC 63.6. CF 31:166.

a) *We have to hit him really hard*

Isaac recognized that there are two men in him, and that they fight each other. **William** cites, in his *Mirror of Faith*, the text of the epistle to the Romans, where the Apostle speaks of the two men who live in him and each pull him in a different direction; it is a struggle: "The flesh struggles against the spirit, and the spirit against the flesh," says Saint Paul again in his epistle to the Galatians.[41] William notes that this state lasts until death. Here below, concupiscence cannot disappear completely, and love cannot become perfect:

> As long as [a person] lives here, carnal yearning can be restrained and broken, but it cannot be so extinguished that it does not exist at all.
>
> For this reason we are commanded in this life to have that perfect love which is unstinting and, according to the precept of the law, which we owe to the Lord God. Yet, no one entirely succeeds in reaching [this love]. It is commanded, all the same, lest we ignore the end toward which we must exert ourselves. The more perfect charity becomes in us, the more necessary it becomes that the flesh be lessened until it [charity] be perfected there, where there is no yearning for anything but God.[42]

Baldwin, who must have had a temper, reporting on an episode in the life of Samuel,[43] engages not only in killing the old man, but in chopping him to pieces:

> When this sword persecutes the old man [in us], it is not satisfied with just killing him: it slices up whomever it kills, cuts him to pieces, and reaches to the division of joints and marrow, until the body of sin is totally destroyed. So it was that the sword of Samuel did not only kill the obese Agag but cut him to pieces.[44]

This same Baldwin, in another tractate, the Eleventh, "On the Crucifixion of our Old Man," personifies this old man. He is

41. Gal 5:17.
42. William, Spec car; PL 180:368D–369A; CF 15:11.
43. 1 Sm 15:23.
44. Baldwin, Tract 6; CF 39:167.

the enemy of Christ, he is the one who demanded his death of Pilate; therefore it is necessary to take vengeance on him. Here, there is no question of loving your enemy:

> The ill-will which the earthly man bears toward Christ has still not passed away, for he persecutes Christ in us to prevent Christ from living in us. If, then, anyone belongs to Christ, let him arm himself with vengeful zeal against those who persecute Christ. For the sake of Christ, let us cry out to each other against the enemy of Christ: "Take him away, take him away! Crucify him!" But what accusation do we bring against this man? "Behold the man that did not make God his helper! He trusted in the abundance of his riches and found his strength in his vanity."[45] "Take him away, take him away! Crucify him!" If you release this man, you are not God's friend.[46] Do to him what he has done! He crucified [Christ]; crucify him! He deserves the cross and is guilty of death![47]

Baldwin goes into the details: he thinks that the cross, for this earthly man, will be formed of two crosspieces: the despising of earthly goods and the despising of the glory of the world. The monks, and we might add all Christians worthy of the name, ought to stretch that man on the cross:

> The earthly man certainly loves these two things, for he trusts in his own strength and glories in the abundance of his riches. He trusts in the world, let it deliver him if it can!
>
> Let those who despise the world stretch [the earthly man] out on the cross. Stretch him out completely, vertically and laterally! Since his height[48] is his earthly glory, [a glory] in which he seeks to be raised [ever higher], let his height be stretched out by a contempt for earthly glory—that is, by voluntary abasement; and since his breadth is his earthly substance, which he seeks to extend to both left and right, let his breadth be stretched out by a contempt for earthly substance—that is, by voluntary poverty.[49]

45. Ps 52.
46. Jn 18:29.
47. Mt 26:66. Baldwin, Tract 11; CF 41:101.
48. French *hauteur*, meaning both "height" and "pride."
49. Baldwin, Tract 11; CF 41:101.

b) *We must trust in grace*

William of Saint-Thierry writes these suggestive lines in his *Exposition on the Epistle to the Romans*:

> For when we were in the flesh, the passions of sins which existed through the law worked in our members to bring forth fruit unto death. . . .
>
> Your concupiscence conquered you, O man, because it found you in a bad place, that is, in the flesh. Leave the flesh. Living in the flesh, do not desire to be in the flesh, but exist in the spirit. What does it mean, "exist in the spirit"? Put your hope in God. . . . Do not put your hope in yourself, but in him who made you. He is your life, and whatever fruit you bear for him, you bear for your own life.[50]

Aelred, in a *Sermon for the First Sunday of Advent* (in his days, on that Sunday, they read the gospel of the triumphal entry of Jesus into Jerusalem), wanted the monks to be like the children of the Hebrews who acclaimed Jesus: they ought to be humble, to force themselves to go beyond the flesh—which presupposes a battle—, by good thoughts, by leaps of contemplation. They struggle against vices, against the devil, against the flesh.[51]

We must ask the Lord to take serious measures to kill our old man: our efforts are necessary, but they are laughable. Only grace enables us to triumph over ourselves. We find here self-forgetfulness, passing from self to God, the work of grace in us.

John of Ford exhorts us to leave the constrictions of the poverty of our soul, to walk in the goodness of Jesus:

> How long, O my soul, will you be disturbed within your self all day, shut up in the narrowness of your personal poverty? Is not the Lord your God . . . himself your beauty, your flower, your lily?[52]

A bit later **John**, in this same commentary on the Song, speaks beautifully of the fire of Jesus: it ought to burn in our very self:

50. William, Exp Rm; PL 180:614B–C; CF 27:133.
51. Aelred, Adv 1, 48–55; PL 195:219C–220A. CF 58:73–75.
52. John, SC 5.1; CF 29:126–127.

> Who will give us of that fire, very fierce yet very gentle. . . . Who
> will at least give each of us one single living and life-giving
> ember, inflaming and melting?

He speaks again of his personal case:

> In the presence of this fire may my heart become like melting
> wax! May my soul faint away before your salvation,[53] Lord,
> may all of me faint, even my eyes, so that it is no longer I
> that live, but Christ who lives in me![54]

Farther on, he considers that his justice to himself is nothing
but a misery; he does not want to think any more except of the
justice of Jesus which becomes his own: it is a sort of huge
seamless cloak which covers his soul.[55]

In the last part of his commentary, in the *One Hundred Sixth
Sermon*, he speaks of the rapport that exists between death and
love: the more we die, the more love will grow. He reproaches
himself for having his old man still so lively; he begs Jesus to
kill him! Jesus has a sword, which gives life and death at the
same time. Taking the word of Saul, which he puts then in
Jonathan's mouth, he does not want to be killed by the sword of
the uncircumcised, but by that of Jesus:

> But I feel great distress for myself—*væ misero mihi*—,
> knowing as I do that the spirit of the old man is still alive
> within me, even to the present day. To a large extent I feel
> it is still master of my senses and affections . . . [L]et me
> not feel the hand of the uncircumcized upon me. No let it
> be you, O Lord, with your mighty sword, dealing out death
> and life, let it be you, I beg, who will kill me.[56]

To evict the old man who is, so to speak, living in our guts,
we must choose our leverage point well: not ourselves, but the
Lord Jesus. **Saint Bernard** said it in energetic terms, in a *Sermon
for Christmas Eve*:

53. Cf. Ps 119.
54. John, SC 7.7; CF 29:159.
55. John, SC 8.6; CF 29:169.
56. John, SC 106.11; CF 47:75.

> Abandon yourself then to God, trust in him, cast on him all your thoughts, he will nourish you, and you can cry to yourself: "The Lord takes care of me."[57]
>
> Putting your trust in yourself is not trust, but treason; to have faith in yourself is the opposite of faith and not trust. The true man of faith is the one who does not believe in himself, who does not hope in himself, who is a piece of trash in his own mind, and loses his soul, but in such a way as to keep it for eternity. For it is only a heart full of humility which can do that, which prevents the faithful soul from counting on itself, and forces it to leave itself, to lift itself at last as from the desert, resting on its Beloved, and from that time, be inundated with delights.[58]

Jesus is truly the new Man, but it is not enough to say that. He also renews others, gives them the power to be new men. It is he, not ourselves, who can work this marvelous conversion, to change our old men into new. In the following lines, Bernard begins by being neutral, but we quickly understand that it is a matter of a person, and nothing less than Jesus:

> He who unceasingly renews our thoughts is always new, and he who does not stop bearing fruit without ever exhausting himself, is never old. For such is the Holy One to whom it is given to never know corruption, such is the new Man who, far from being capable of growing old, gives a true youth full of life to those who have grown old down to the marrow of their bones.[59]

Because Jesus lives in his disciple, the old man must die in him. Who can really make him die? At the end of a certain time of generous struggle (which was necessary) we find it out: we are incapable ourselves, the Lord himself must get into the battle. Also, in prayer we ask him not to worry, to go ahead and destroy by the trials he chooses (in the moment when he gives his grace) this bad nature, this old man, these unregulated passions. Who would not make the words of **Guerric** his own?

57. Ps 40.
58. Sg 8:5. Bernard, V Nat 5.5.
59. Bernard, V Nat 6.6.

We know how great is the multitude of your sweetness, Lord, which you have hidden from those that fear you[60] and will grant in abundance to them who hope in you. And I shall always hope, even if you were to kill me.[61] Indeed I shall hope all the more when you scourge, lash, burn, kill all that lives in me, so that not I but Christ may live in me.[62]

60. Ps 31.
61. Jb 13:15.
62. Guerric, Ben 1.4; CF 32:5.

VII   BEING SMALL

Dom Chautard was astonished by the retreat given by Father Godefroid Bélorgey in 1930. After a teaching, when the preacher had already left the room, and while we were still all on our knees in prayerful silence, he stood up alone, to share his admiration with us. "There at last, my dear brothers, we have a retreat completely centered on the presence of God, just as I wanted. Last year I had already requested it, but the preacher only gave us a mosaic!"

Fr Godefroid had insisted a great deal on the energy that we must put forth to arrive at union with God, at contemplation. "There are unsuspected energies in a man who desires," he said. I told myself, "I do not *want* to occupy myself with anything but God!" A short time after the retreat, Dom Chautard came to the novitiate. He expressed again to us his admiration for the retreat, and he added a caution: not to count too much on the will. Contemplation is above all a matter of grace: we must do our part, but be small, not count on anything but grace to arrive at that habitual and "loving" remembrance of God. I added then to my first thought, "My God, I do not want to occupy myself with anything but you," this second: "I come to you like a little child. I will do what I can, since you want it, but it's laughable; it's you who do everything."

Watch out, because pride, in more or less subtle forms, lies in wait for us. This may be:

• a secret self-esteem (phariseeism): I am not like the others who fail at silence, become impatient, love to eat, etc.
• ambition: to come to have a position of responsibility in the monastery. This happened even in the times of our first Fathers. **Aelred** cites the monks who sigh:

O if I were abbot,—or prior or cellarer or porter, I would
not involve myself in earthly matters. I would do this and
that—*hoc facerem et illud*—.[1]

These are the "machinations of their hearts," he said.

•susceptibility, "the capital sin of Church people," said Fr
Godefroid, which translates into inexpiable rancor. He called to
mind the famous "Papal mule," of the tales of Daudet . . .

All that comes when one has an exaggerated opinion of
oneself, when one takes as one's own what God has given us.
"What do you have that you have not received?" said Saint
Paul.[2]

In leaning on the texts of our Fathers, we are going to propose
and expose the following ideas:

It is necessary to be small like the baby Jesus.
God loves little ones. The Spirit of God rests on the little ones.
To have a humble opinion of oneself.
To depend on nothing but God.

1) Being small like the baby Jesus

God could have come to this world and taken our humanity
without passing through the smallness, the weakness, and even
the friendliness of infancy. He chose to come through Mary. How
strongly **Saint Bernard** repeats it: "Such was the will of God. He
wanted everything to come to us through Mary. I repeat: such
was his will."[3]

He is lovable. Transposing a phrase from the Psalms: "The
Lord is great and infinitely worthy of praise,"[4] **Bernard** has this
delicious phrase:

Little is the Lord and greatly to be loved.[5]

1. Aelred, PP 17.9; PL 195.296A; CF 58.248.
2. 1 Cor 4:7.
3. Bernard, Nat BVM, 7.
4. Ps 48.
5. Bernard, SC 48.3; CF 31:14.

This little child wants to be respected and loved, but also imitated. In his *Sermon on Conversion to the Clergy*, **Bernard** speaks to them of "conversion": they must become like tiny babies. Jesus said: "If you do not become like these little children, you will not enter into the Kingdom of Heaven"[6]:

> Certainly, because only the little children enter, since it is a little child who leads them, he who was born for us and who was given to us precisely for that purpose.[7]

Guerric says explicitly that this little child whom it is necessary to be like is Jesus himself. Men, with their pride, act like giants; they must lose their stature to enter into the Kingdom of God:

> O sweet and sacred childhood, which brought back man's true innocence, by which men of every age can return to blessed childhood and be conformed to you, not in physical weakness, but in humility of heart and holiness of life.
>
> In a word then you sons of Adam, who are exceedingly great in your own eyes and have grown by pride into giants, unless you are converted and become like this little Child, you shall not enter into the kingdom of Heaven. "I am the Gate of the Kingdom," this little Child says, and unless man's proud head is bowed the doorway of humility will not let him in.[8]

Bernard also has the same idea: it is necessary to become like that little child *who is Jesus*, it is necessary to turn back (which is what the word "convert" means). In his *Second Sermon for Ash Wednesday*, he begins with the text from Joel used in the liturgy of the day: "*Convertimini*—Return to me with all your heart. . . ."[9] What does this commandment of the Lord to turn toward him mean? It is everywhere . . . It is a secret that is not revealed except to his friends: if you do not turn back to become *like a*

---

6. Mt 18:3.
7. Bernard, Conv, 1.
8. Guerric, Nat 1.2; SC 166.169; CF 8:38–39.
9. Jl 2:12.

little child, you will not enter into the Kingdom of Heaven, and Bernard continues:

> I understand perfectly what we need to turn toward (turn back to): we must turn back to (turn to) this Little one, so that we can learn from him that he is sweet and humble of heart; he was given to us as a baby just for that. O man, why do you puff up yourself? Why do you raise yourself up without reason? Why those thoughts of grandeur, and those looks always directed toward that which is lifted up and which cannot be good for you? Of course the Lord is great, but that is not how he has set you an example. We must praise his grandeur, but not imitate it at all. The Lord is lifted up, he looks at what is lowly,[10] and does not regard one who lifts himself up except from a distance. *Abase yourself, and you have already understood—humiliare et apprehendisti.*[11]

In his *Second Sermon for the Conversion of Saint Paul*, **Bernard** gives us the same teaching, but in an even more explicit fashion: the little child that Jesus gives us to imitate is himself:

> Today Saul is converted into Paul. He has become like the little child of the gospel, of whom the Lord said: "If you do not change and become like this little child, you will not enter into the Kingdom of Heaven." Maybe it was of himself that the Lord spoke, because he, the Lord, great beyond measure, and worthy of all praises, was given to us as a tiny baby. He did not show himself great to our eyes, but tiny, to give us in his person an example as agreeable as it is efficacious of a necessary humility.
>
> Turn toward this little child, to learn how to become a little child; for once you have turned (converted), you will become a little child.[12]

2) God loves children; the Spirit of God rests on little children

Such is his taste; that is how he looks at things. I knew very well a certain Sister Seraphine, who died at age forty-seven. The

---

10. Those who are humble: the "humilia respicit" of the *Magnificat* and Ps 138.

11. Bernard, Cin 2.1.

12. Bernard, Pl 2.1.

day before her death, as she was completely overcome by the knowledge of her own unworthiness, I said to her (and it was quite true, because the Lord had showered her poverty with grace): "The good God loves you very much," to which she replied without hesitation, "Oh well, he doesn't have very good taste!"

It is the taste of God to choose and to favor the more humble. The Virgin chose to appear to children, Bernadette, Diego, Catherine Labouré, the little children of Pontmain or of Fátima. The Virgin Mary attests to it herself: "He has regarded the low estate of his handmaiden."

He more often chose the second than the first: Abel, Jacob; he chose the last: Saul, David. For his people, he is careful to warn:

> If Yahweh is attached to you and has chosen you, it is not because you are the most numerous of all peoples, but it is for love of you, because you are the least among all nations.[13]

> Yahweh, my heart is not proud nor my regard haughty,
> I have not taken a road of grandeur,
> Nor prodigies which are too high for me.
> No, I hold my soul in peace and in silence,
> Like a small child against its mother,
> Like a small child, is my soul within me.[14]

> That which is taken for foolishness in the world,
> God has chosen to confound the wise;
> that which is weak in the world,
> God has chosen to confound the strong;
> that which in the world is without lineage,
> and despised, which is nothing,
> God has chosen in order to reduce to nothing that which is,
> so that no fleshly thing should have anything to boast about before
> God.[15]

Therefore our personal "goods," qualities, gifts, virtues, and charisms belong to all. On this point **Baldwin of Ford** in his tractate *On the Cenobitic or Common Life* has some arresting ideas

13. Dt 7:7.
14. Ps 131.
15. 1 Cor 1:27–28.

and some trenchant affirmations. It goes without saying that a gift received from God does not keep its worth as a true good unless it is shared, or at least possessed without an ownership mentality. That supposes an outstanding humility.[16]

Since the Lord insists so much that we should become like little children, we could ask different people to reflect on and describe what each one thinks is *the humility of children*. Here is what I have thought that I could respond to such a question:

The special kind of humility of children

1) *They accept being treated as nothing at all*

We take no account of manners, do not "wear gloves" in saying certain things to a small child to reprove it, as one would with older people: "Get out of there, you are embarrassing me!" You wouldn't say that to a big boy, or a big girl; if you said it to them, it would offend, do harm, or wound.

It is in fact a great virtue to be able to accept being treated any which way, by no matter whom, no matter when, without losing one's peace nor one's personality; because it is not at all a matter of becoming a cipher! But let's listen to the counsels of a "Little Thérèse" who knew how to accept humiliating events, by the grace of God, and nevertheless develop her personality:

> Above all we should be so small, so very small that the whole world could trample us underfoot, without seeming that we notice it at all.

Mother Marie de Jésus, the foundress of the Carmel of Paray-le-Monial, gave this advice to her religious:

> Each of us should be in such a state that I and nothing are the same thing; then anything that touches that nothing, is itself nothing.[17]

We could cite here the words of **William of Saint-Thierry**:

---

16. Baldwin, Tract 15, CF 41:156–191, esp. 185–186.
17. Une carmélite de Paray, *Vie de Mère Marie de Jésus*, 70.

But there is a more sublime humility which looks for the reward of perfection; it consists in being submissive to one's inferior and preferring one's equal to oneself for God's sake, not merely by the judgment of reason, but by impulse of conscience.[18]

We also quote a passage from the tractate of **Baldwin of Ford** *On Beatitudes in the Gospel*, in the pages that he dedicates to the beatitude, and later to the virtue, of sweetness:

Who are the infants and sucklings? Who but the little ones, the humble, the simple, the meek, the docile, the patient, and those who do not overcome good with evil but overcome evil with good.[19]

An infant is one who utters no word (*in-fans*) and a suckling one who sucks milk. But listen to an infant speaking: "I set a guard upon my mouth when the sinner stood against me." If he is cursed, he does not curse [in return], and if he is beaten, he does not utter threats. When he is injured, he is silent and says, "I became like a man who does not hear, who has no reproofs in his mouth."[20]

We visualize the scene that Walter Daniel, monk of Rievaulx, sketches of his holy abbot **Aelred**:

His graciousness and good will were so great that injury did not stir him up to anger, nor slander provoke him to vengeance . . . and the serenity of his own peaceable heart lit up, in contrast, the disordered mind of the ill-wisher.[21]

2) *They are dependent, they are conscious of their incapacity, they find it completely natural not to be able to do things*

There is a natural tendency that is profoundly anchored in man: to want not to be dependent on anyone else. How many people have a hard time accepting the diminution that age imposes on them: not to be able to do physically or intellectually

---

18. William, Cant 8.108; CF 6:87.
19. Rom 12:21.
20. Ps 38. Baldwin, Tract 9; CF 41:37.
21. Walter, Vita Ael, 2; CF 57:92.

what they used to do easily. A humility of spiritual childhood rejoices in not being able to do things.

Saint Bernard went so far as to rejoice when someone did not follow a piece of advice that he had requested of him;[22] he hoped to be made ridiculous:

> Play the mountebank I will and humble myself in my own esteem—*ludam ut illudar*.

We could translate in a slightly vulgar way, but one that accurately portrays the thought of the saint:

> I shall play the mountebank that I may be mocked.[23]

3) *They have a liberty and even an impudence that one would not tolerate in older people*

As it has been said, a small child can pull his grandfather's beard just for fun; he could not do it a few years later without being corrected.

To be audacious in his prayer, while speaking with the Father or with Jesus. To reflect his own words back to him: "You have only to ask!"

> Is it nothing to you that I perish?
> Whatever you want to do, do it quickly!

To remind him of the word that he has spoken, in the parable of the workers sent to the vineyard: "Do I not have the right to do what I want with my own possessions?" To add: my soul, that concerns you! You can do what you want, make me want . . . .

When as we gaze at the tabernacle, we ask him to take us and tell him that we wish to give ourselves to him, and he does not seem to pay attention, the little child may be so bold as to say: "If it were the devil who was in the tabernacle—God forgive me!—and I said that to him, I wouldn't have to say it twice! He would take charge of me right away!"

22. Bernard, Epp 90.11 (Cist ed 87); James, 134.
23. Bernard, Epp 90.12 (Cist ed 87); James, 135.

In short, these are simple words, as Saint Thérèse of the Child Jesus would say, but words that touch the heart of the Master.

God loves little children. Alluding to Psalm 116, **Aelred,** in a sermon for Advent, speaks of the little children who acclaimed Jesus in the temple:

> *The Lord keeps watch over little ones.* For he keeps watch, not over the great and the exalted and the proud, but over the *little ones*—that is, the humble. They it is who praise the Lord, provided they are Hebrews—that is, *those who leap (transilientes).*[24]
>
> If now they are humble, if now they forego the deeds and the vices of the flesh, if now they know how to take spiritual leaps through contemplation and through good thoughts, then on the day of judgement, when Jesus comes in his power, they will, without doubt, come *to meet him* with palms—that is, with the insignia of the victories that they have won here over the devil.[25]

God reveals himself to the little ones, to those who remain tranquil. Our Fathers had a special fondness for the phrase that they read in their Bible: "Upon whom will my spirit rest, if not on the humble, the peaceful, on the one who venerates the words of the Lord?"[26] Among a number of others, here is a passage from **William:**

> Hasten to be partakers of the Holy Spirit then, He is present when he is invoked and he will not help unless he is invoked. When invoked, he comes; he comes in the abundance of God's blessing. He is the torrent of the river making happy the city of God. And if, when he shall come, he finds you humble and quiet and fearing the words of God, he will rest upon you and he will reveal to you what God the Father withdraws from the wise and prudent of this world. Those things which Wisdom was able to teach the disciples on earth will begin to enlighten you.[27]

24. Fr Thomas translates as "People of Passage."
25. Aelred, Adv 1; PL 195.219D; CF 58:75.
26. Is 66:2.
27. William, Spec fid; PL 180.384B–C; CF 15:54.

It is so good to think that God reveals himself to the children! Jesus rejoiced in it, he experienced a bounding in his heart, analogous to that of the holy Virgin in her Magnificat.

Nothing more than to forget oneself in order to think only of God, this is not an easy spirituality, this being small: it is a passage, it is a small death.

3) Having a humble opinion of self

There is no place for being proud. When we appear before God in prayer, we do not come with raised head, but with the simplicity of a child: "I am indigent and poor" we say with the psalmist.[28] It is our ticket to prayer!

In the intimacy of our heart, we should address ourselves sometimes: "You are not a Christian, a daughter of God, a monk!"

Saint Bernard humbled himself: "An unfledged nestling, I am obliged to spend most of my time out of my nest"[29]; "a sort of modern chimera, neither cleric nor layman."[30]

Guerric said for his part:

> Rightly then this religious habit which I wear, to which is added almost no witness of virtue, fills me with both shame and fear. For can I safely take to myself the name and honor of a monk when I do not possess its merit and virtue; since, as has been said before our time, an affected sanctity is a double iniquity, and the wolf that is caught in sheep's clothing is to be condemned all the more severely?[31]

Here is what **William** thinks of himself before God, in his prayer, according to what he wrote in his *Twelfth Meditation*:

> Even as the truth is present with yourself, my will is set to call on you in truth today. Hear me therefore, O Truth, in the

---

28. Ps 70.
29. Bernard, Epp 13 (Cist ed 12); James, 49.
30. Bernard, Epp 326 (Cist ed 250.4); James, 402.
31. Guerric, Epi 4, 2–3; CF 8:93; cf. SCh 166.293.

multitude of your mercy and in the truth of your salvation. For I said: "Now I have begun. Be this your change, O right hand of the highest." For my past sins and evils, which are great, inveterate and numberless, have made me vile and despicable to myself. And, as to my good qualities, if any such have been observed in me, I am most suspicious of them.[32]

To have a humble opinion of yourself . . . It is not necessary to make the change: it is easy to say you are a miserable sinner; you risk believing that in fact you despise yourself, that you are humble. Many times I have heard Dom Chautard declare: "You are sincere, but you are not speaking the truth." Are you speaking the "truth," when you say sincerely that you are a poor sinner, that you are worthless, etc.? There is an easy test: one day or another someone, above all if he is irritated, will reproach you and will tell you more or less explicitly that you are worthless. If, even while experiencing a shock in your feelings, you agree that that is what you yourself think, that is fine, your humble opinion of yourself is true. Fr Jacques Laval who did so much good on the island of Mauritius, had to undergo plenty of humiliations and mockeries. Here is what his reaction was:

> They take me for what I am: for a beast and a good for nothing. Oh! How good and true that is![33]

4) Leaning only on God

God alone can give us a true humility, making us know and feel our true misery:

> Human misery never appears so clearly as it does in the light of the face of God.

That is how **William** expresses himself in his *Golden Epistle*[34]; put another way: when God gives us the grace of a stronger union with him, when we feel esteemed, wrapped in his regard (which

32. William, Med 12.1; CF 3:167.
33. *Vie du P. J. Laval*, 73.
34. William, Ep frat II.18; CF 12:97.

does not lack sweetness!), it is at that very moment that we see ourselves in truth poor and pitiable, and we would not be angry that others should know it, because it is the truth!

Saint Bernard, in his *Thirty-sixth Sermon on the Song*, speaks of the necessity of knowing ourselves; it is the best means of having a humble opinion of yourself. Then he shows, exposing his own case, that that forces us to have recourse to the divine mercy:

> And there is nothing more effective, more adapted to the acquiring of humility, than to find out the truth about oneself. . . . How can he escape being genuinely humbled on acquiring this true self-knowledge, on seeing the burden of sin that he carries, the oppressive weight of his mortal body, the complexities of earthly cares, the corrupting influence of sensual desires . . . . Can this man afford the haughty eyes, the proud lift of the head? . . . Let him be changed and weep, changed to mourning and sighing, changed to acceptance of the Lord, to whom in his lowliness he will say: "Heal me because I have sinned against you."[35]

God, seeing this misery humbly recognized, will show himself merciful:

> He will certainly find consolation in this turning to the Lord, because he is "the Father of mercies and the God of all comfort."[36]

There is where Bernard comes on stage and gives his personal example. He experienced that misery, having evidence of his misery; around him, he could not find any support, so he decided to lean only on God:

> As for me, as long as I look at myself, my eye is filled with bitterness.[37] But if I look up and fix my eyes on the aid of the divine mercy, this happy vision of God soon tempers the bitter vision of myself.[38]

35. Ps 41.
36. 2 Cor 1:3.
37. Jb 17:2.
38. Bernard, SC 36.5–6; CF 7:177–179.

Elsewhere, in his *Fifth Sermon for Christmas Eve*, **Bernard** shows very nicely how it is necessary to have lost confidence in yourself, therefore in the possibility of leaning on yourself, in order to be able truly to place your confidence in God and lean on him:

> Trust in God, put yourself in his hands, cast on him your cares, and he will then nourish you, you will be able to say with filial abandon: "The Lord takes care of me."[39]
>
> Men who love themselves cannot know this, those little evil ones, always turned in on themselves, deaf to the voice of him who said: "Cast on him your cares, because he himself takes care of you."[40]

In his *Third Sermon on Various Subjects*, **Bernard** speaks of the soul that experiences that its good works do not belong to it; they are rather granted it by God; its perfection is brought to completion in its weakness.[41]

Guerric, in his *Fourth Sermon for Christmas*, basing his comments on the phrase of the psalm: "I will remember nothing but your justice,"[42] speaks of the necessity of not leaning on anything but God, of not making ourselves a "law unto ourselves."[43]

Let us cite one last text to close this discussion on passing from self to God by humility and the awareness of our smallness; it is from **John of Ford**:

> These little ones . . . were small and weak in their own eyes, and this is enough to make them very great in yours. They were poor in their own merits, but very rich in your approval! It suffices them for all merit to have found [approval] with you.[44]

---

39. Ps 40.
40. 1 Pt 5:7. Bernard, V Nat 5.5.
41. Bernard, Div 3.2–3.
42. Ps 71.
43. Guerric, Nat 4.2; CF 8:56–57.
44. John, SC 3.2; CF 29:101–102.

VIII   PRAISING GOD

Forget yourself, yes, but in order to occupy yourself with God, not in order to think of any old thing or to extinguish all human desire and enter into a sort of nirvana. Forget yourself, yes, but in order to occupy yourself with God.

To pass from self to God, to think of the divine benefits, to think about what God is, and to bless him, to praise him. In forgetting yourself in order to think of God, try it: you topple inevitably and happily into divine praise. Inevitably you begin to glorify God, to say "Glory to the Father, and to the Son, and to the Holy Spirit . . . ," you have on the tip of your tongue the first words of the "Glory to God in the highest," or other words of pure praise of God, where it is not at all a question of us. And because it is always true, whether you are having a good day or a bad day, you are sure not to make a mistake by praising God for what he is and what he has done. You remember nothing, according to the phrase of the psalm we have already cited, "but the justice of God alone," you have your "mouth filled with his praise."

Elisabeth of the Trinity, in her *Élévation* asked God to "forget herself completely"; she wanted also "to be a praise of glory." The two things are related.

Aelred, in a sermon for Lent, after having spoken of fasting and almsgiving, adds:

> Then that man, purified by such a fast, reinvigorated (*recreatus*) by such an almsgiving, has nothing more to do than to enter into the chamber of his heart, then, after having closed the door of all bodily senses, to allow his soul to expand within him and to pass into the admirable place

of the sanctuary, as far as the house of God, *with cries of exultation and of praise.*[1]

You recollect yourself, enter into the chamber of your heart, but it is in order to pass from there to the heavens and to rejoice in God.

To leave yourself in that way (or, which amounts to the same thing, to enter deeply into yourself to recollect yourself in God), to leave yourself to praise God, *that is what best represents our eternal occupation in heaven,* it is already to begin our heaven. Here again we rejoin the *Élévation* of blessed Elisabeth who wanted to establish herself already in eternity in order to praise God here below.

Saint Bernard, in an admirable passage of his *Commentary on the Song*, invites his brothers to exult in thanksgiving: it is what best represents life in heaven, and he promises that it also makes life here below more tolerable:

> I long to see you all sharing in that holy anointing, that religious attitude in which the benefits of God are recalled with gladness and thanksgiving. This involves a twofold grace: it lightens the burdens of the present life, makes them more supportable for those who can give themselves with joy to the work of praising God; and nothing more appropriately represents on earth the state of life in the heavenly fatherland than spontaneity in this outpouring of praise. Scripture implies as much when it says: "Happy those who live in your house and can praise you all day long."[2]

The saint adds that praising God in that way in a divine office, in a liturgical assembly, is a community "confession," since when we remember our sins, it is a "confession" which is not communitarian, common: each one weeps for his own sins:

> Those . . . who are employed (*versantur*) in the work of thanksgiving are contemplating and thinking about God alone.

1. Ps 42. Aelred, SI 6.62.
2. Ps 84. Bernard, SC 11.1; CF 4:69.

That is the point that he pursues, in inviting his brothers to forget from time to time (I would willingly say as often as possible, every time the thought comes to our spirit) their own miseries as sinners, to lose themselves in the smoother roads of remembering the benefits of God, of the "gentleness" (*benignitatis*) of God. This lets us inhale a gust of good air, we breathe: *ipsius intuitu respiretis.*

The double confession

There is the confession of sins, and also that of the benefits or the goodness of God. Let me cite two passages from **Saint Bernard**, both taken from his *Sermons on Various Subjects*:

> Confession is a good ornament for the soul: it purifies the sinner and renders the just purer. If there are sins, they are washed away by confession; if there are good actions, they become more precious through confession [of praise]. When you confess your sins, you offer to God the sacrifice of a broken heart; when you confess the benefits of God, you raise up to him a sacrifice of praise.[3]

We often find in the Psalms the confession of sins and that of the goodness of God:

> We find a double confession in the psalmody: that of sins which fills the sinner with compunction; that of praises which one addresses to God because of his just judgments.[4]

Here now is another text of **Bernard**, but this one drawn from his *Commentary on the Song*, apropos of the verse: "There he is behind the wall, gazing through the windows, looking through the lattices"[5]; he recommends keeping both the windows and the lattices completely open. The lattices (*cancelli*) are narrow openings: that is the confession of sins; the Lord looks through these little openings, because he loves a contrite heart; but the

---

3. Ps 50. Bernard, Div 40.2.
4. Bernard, Div 55.1.
5. Sg 2:9.

big windows are the praises of God which leap from the heart, and the Lord looks through these openings with even greater pleasure:

> If at times, when the heart expands in love at the thought of God's graciousness and mercy, it is all right to surrender our mind, to let it go in songs of praise and gratitude, I feel that I have opened up to the Bridegroom who stands behind the wall not a narrow lattice but a wide-open window. Through it, unless I am mistaken, he will look in with greater pleasure the more he is honored by the sacrifice of praise.[6]

Isaac of Stella, in a *Sermon for the Third Sunday of Lent*, lists three ways our tongue uses to address God:

—when it praises God
—when it accuses itself before God
—when it edifies our neighbor

The person who keeps silence on these three points is truly mute, in spite of his cries:

> O Lord Jesus, chase away my demon! Open my lips for a humble confession of my sins so that my mouth may worthily announce your praises! Otherwise praise will not be beautiful in the mouth of a sinner.[7] "You have garbed yourself in praise (of confession) and in beauty."[8]

Helinand, the former troubadour become a monk of Froidmont, in a sermon for Palm Sunday, said that it is necessary to glorify God in three ways:

> By the mouth, by the heart, by exterior works. By the heart in believing, by the mouth in confessing, by works in triumphing over our passions.

Here is how he distinguishes the two ways of confessing God; we find again the same distinction the others make:

6. Bernard, SC 56.7; CF 31:93–94.
7. Si 15:9.
8. Ps 104. Isaac, Quad 3; PL 194, 1819C.

There is a double confession, that of sin and that of praise. For example: "We confess you, O God, we confess you!"[9] We confess our sins, we confess your benefits; for God is glorified by these two confessions. Here is the word of Joshua to Achan, who had committed a flight under anathema: "My son, give glory to God, avow what you have done."[10] Here it was a matter of confession of sin. For the confession of praise, there is the song of the angels: "Glory to God in the highest."[11]

The lines which follow are addressed by **Bernard** to his monks of Clairvaux who chanted the divine office every day; but every Christian, every reader of this book will have no trouble in drawing profit from them, if he reflects that as a child of God, he ought according to what Saint Paul says, praise God with his brothers:

May the word of Christ live among you in all its richness; sing to God, in your hearts, your recognition through psalms, hymns, and songs inspired by the Spirit.[12]

Saint Bernard is persuaded that the life of a monk (let us say also the life of any Christian, in another form) ought to be a life of praise; he makes an effort to persuade his religious at Clairvaux of this. Here is how, for example, he commented to them on this word of the liturgy of the day, in a sermon for Christmas Eve:

"O Judah and Jerusalem, do not be afraid!"[13] No, do not be afraid, you who are true confessors, who confess the Lord not only with your mouth but with your whole being, and who make of confession your clothing; even better, "whose interior parts confess the Lord,"[14] you "whose bones say: Lord, who is like you?"[15]

9. Ps 75. The RSV has "we give thanks to you."
10. Jos 7:19.
11. Helinand, Palm 5; PL 212, 584B.
12. Col 3:16.
13. 2 Chr 20:17.
14. Ps 103.
15. Ps 35.

But these words are not addressed to those who confess the Lord with their mouth, and deny him by their works.[16] Your confession will be true, brothers, on condition that all your works are his works, and that you confess him. For it is necessary that you confess him in two ways, and that you be dressed in a double vestment, by the confession of your sins, and by the confession of the Lord which consists in singing his praises.[17]

Yes, praising God is essential. **Bernard** addressed these words again to his monks at the end of his *Tenth Sermon on the Song*, when he came to speak of the ardor of the apostles who exulted in having suffered for the name of Jesus:

How I wish . . . that I might see you men rich in virtue, prompt to sing God's praises.[18]

If we read the beginning of the *First Sermon for Christmas Eve* or the *Third* and the *Fifth for Ascension Day*, we will feel that same communicative flame: **Bernard** is an enthusiast for God, and he wants to share that enthusiasm.

At first the sinner cannot praise the Lord in beauty—again this same text from Sirach: "The praise of God is not beautiful in the mouth of the sinner"[19]; but, freed of his sin:

Sharing the benefits of God, he adheres to the divine praise, he experiences its delights and progresses so well in that exercise that nothing pleases him more; then the praise of God in his mouth is beautiful![20]

Thanksgiving; the remembrance of the divine benefits

The praise of God, thanksgiving for his benefits, these two elevations of the soul are very close together and frequently are mixed with each other. We praise God for what he is and for

16. Ti 1:16.
17. Bernard, V Nat 2.1.
18. Bernard, SC 10.10; CF 4:68.
19. Si 15:9.
20. Bernard, Div 81.

what he does; we thank him for what he does or for what he is: "We thank you for your immense glory," we say in the *Gloria in excelsis*.

Already, in what has been said here about praise, we have encountered texts which speak of the divine benefits; in particular that from the *Eleventh Sermon of* **Saint Bernard** *on the Song*, where the saint invites his brothers to forget from time to time the remembrance of "their own ways" which are difficult, to wander on the smoother roads of the remembrance of the divine benefits: it is to leave yourself to praise God.

Evidently one can find a nuance between the two practices of praise and of thanksgiving; we can see it perhaps better considering their opposites: murmuring, discontent, turning back into self which are truly opposed to praise; ingratitude, forgetfulness of benefits which are opposed to thanksgiving and gratefulness.

Here is a text where we find the two aspects, ingratitude and the lack of praise. It is from **John of Ford**. In his *Hundred First Sermon on the Song*, he speaks of the first sin, that of Adam and Eve; he sees in it the cause, the origin in their ingratitude: made in the image of God, they ought to have thanked him, to have blessed him because they were privileged among all the creatures. They failed to recognize it.

The devil cased the house and realized that it was empty of praise (*a laude Dei vacantem invenit*). He remembered his own fall, how while the stars of the dawn and all the sons of God rejoiced, he himself kept his mouth shut and stayed mute instead of praising God, he and all the accomplices of his pride, he was expelled with good reason from the choir, from the "assembly of those who praise God." He noticed then that man could fall into the same trap.[21]

Saint Bernard saw curiosity as the spur to the first sin; John of Ford saw lack of praise.

Clearly, you should not compare such an explication of original sin with the current explanations of exegetes or theologians who make an effort to shed some light on something

---

21. John, SC 101.2; CF 47:3.

which remains a mystery. It is not a matter here of judging an explanation which might seem infantile, but of inclining your intellect and reading while praying. At bottom, in all sin, we find something of man's pride, of his ingratitude in the face of the God of love. We recoil, become quiet, humble ourselves, when we recognize in ourselves traces of pride and ingratitude.

We have a whole sermon of **Saint Bernard** on the vice of ingratitude: the *Twenty-seventh on Various Subjects*. The holy abbot begins by putting us face to face with the immense mercy which has uprooted us from the world in which we lived as those "without God" or those "against God," from blindness or perversity. He exposes in a few phrases the double mercy of God for those whom he has called to the monastic life: he has not only drawn us from the world, but also put us in the cloister, which is a considerable favor:

> If we consider attentively not only where he drew us from, but still more where we have been placed, we will certainly not fail to find that the treasures of the second mercy are worth even more than those of the first. God has not acted like this with all men. He has treated us magnificently, not only in taking us as his servitors, but in choosing us for his friends.[22]

No one would deny, I suppose, everyone will comprehend that a nun or a monk can bless God for her or his vocation. But on the one side, he or she ought to watch out not to glory in what has been received as if it had been earned, and on the other, the fact of being a baptized Christian easily permits any person to consider himself or herself not only as a servitor, but also a friend, an intimate friend of Jesus, a son or daughter of God. "Go, daughter of God!" said the Voices to Joan of Arc. Every Christian, if he listens to the murmur or the cry of the Holy Spirit hears, and murmurs or cries from the depth of his heart: "Abba! Father!"

Everything that we have received from God ought to flow back to him in thanksgiving. Here is how **Bernard** tells us again:

> Let the rivers of grace circle back to their Fountain-Head that they may run their course anew. Let the torrent that

22. Bernard, Div 27.1.

springs in heaven be channelled back to its starting point,
and be poured on the earth again with fertilizing power. You
ask how this will be done. It will be done in accord with
Paul's advice: "In all things give thanks to God."[23]

Still more formal is the teaching that **Bernard** gives again
on this point, in another sermon on the Song:

> Learn to not be tardy or sluggish in offering thanks, learn
> to offer thanks for each and every gift . . . . Ingratitude
> is the soul's enemy, a voiding of merits, dissipation of the
> virtues, wastage of benefits. Ingratitude is a burning wind
> that dries up the source of love, the dew of mercy, the
> streams of grace.[24]

A passage of **William**, in his *Exposition on the Song*, is very
appropriate for causing us to reflect, so well has he expressed
things. It is a matter of seeing yourself in truth before God, of
not lifting yourself up proudly, of recognizing without doubt the
value which you have, but in returning to God, by recognition
[thanksgiving], what we hold from him:

> To yourself you seem of little worth, but in reality you are
> precious. Insofar as you forsook him whose image you are,
> you have taken on the colors of strange images. But when
> you begin to breathe in the atmosphere wherein you were
> created, if perchance you embrace discipline, you will quickly
> shake off and renounce this false make-up which is only
> superficial and not even skin-deep. Be wholly present to
> yourself, therefore, and employ yourself wholly in knowing
> yourself and knowing whose image you are, and likewise in
> discerning and understanding what you are and what you
> can do in him whose image you are. Stand in your rank; be not
> overcome, be not dishonored. The strength of your position
> is the knowledge of grace, if you are not ungrateful that you
> were foreseen, predestined, preferred and foreknown.[25]

William, always fascinated by the face of God, by the
experience, the mystical attainment of God, sees more than once,

23. 1 Thes 5:18. Bernard, SC 13.1; CF 4:87–88.
24. Bernard, SC 51.6; CF 31:44–45.
25. William, Cant 1.5; CF 6:53.

in the recognition of the divine benefits, a road which leads by the way of love to that experiential attainment of God, to what we would call a grace of union. So this passage from the same commentary on the Song:

> For whenever a soul receives, by God's gift, a certain grace for its own profit, it receives also, with that gift, understanding of the Giver; that man may not be ungrateful to God, but his turning may be toward the Giver. When humble love turns toward God more ardently, it is conformed to him toward whom it turns; because as it turns it is given by him an aptitude for such conformity. And since man is made in the likeness of his Maker, he becomes attracted to God; that is, he becomes one spirit with God, beautiful in his Beauty, good in his Goodness; and this takes place in proportion to the strength of his faith, the light of his understanding and the measure of his love. He is then in God, by grace, what God is by nature.[26]

Merlin Carothers, a Protestant pastor, wrote two little books that are valuable and have had an extraordinarily large distribution: *From Prison to Praise* and *The Power of Praise*. Little by little he got into the habit, based on the Scripture, especially Saint Paul, of blessing, of thanking God in everything, no matter how annoying the circumstances. He managed to find people in the middle of circumstances which were humanly speaking catastrophic, had them get on their knees and, in an admirable act of faith, bless God for what had just happened to them. I propose three little formulas to say sincerely in the small or large daily trials. To those who are willing to try this I promise peace and joy, peace and joy from God!

> —This comes from the Father, it is good!
> —This pleases you, it pleases me.
> And above all, because it is truly applicable in all cases:
> —This figures in your grand plan of love for me, blessed
>   be you, Father!

If malice from your neighbor interferes, you can hardly use the first two formulas, but the third certainly works. You

26. William, Cant 1.8; CF 6:76.

must recognize that it is not easy, not even possible for men, but everything is possible for God, everything is possible for him who believes; Jesus has said it.[27]

When we have said that, it's over: we don't want to grumble anymore.

Then, in everything we can say and sing with our whole heart "Magnificat!"; to join with the Holy Virgin, to praise with her spirit, as Saint Grignion de Montfort recommends, following Saint Ambrose, can only help and increase our joy.

Let's cite a text of **Gilbert of Hoyland** who speaks of this joy of the soul that lives always in the presence of God, seeing him through all circumstances. It is taken from his *Third Tractate*, which could be called *Earthly Joys and Heavenly Joys*.[28]

In the first paragraph, he developed this thought: all day it is good to stay still before God, to hold yourself in his presence in prayer. In the second, it is the idea that it is also necessary, all day, to follow the Lord. For Gilbert, following him would be already to lead something of a heavenly life. He desires that it should be a joy, not a labor:

> Who will give me the footing of hinds,
> that nimble and keen I may be able to pursue this young hind
> and that, unlearning my household chores,
> I may range the forest in heavenly solitude?
> It is good to shed the heaviest burden,
> the burden of oneself,
> and to be reduced imperceptibly
> to the nimbleness of wild goats.

He adds several scriptural texts that, as for Bernard, designate the goal, the occupation of the monastic life:

> All is enacted within,
> for the song is sung in his heart,
> for there too the race is run.

---

27. Mk 9:23.
28. Entitled in CF34 *How Joy Differs on the Way and in the Fatherland.*

Let us cite the Latin, if only for the assonances:

> Totum intus agitur
> in corde enim canitur
> nam et ibi curritur.

In the third paragraph, he says that it is contemplation which gives joy:

> So delight flows from the light and thanksgiving flows from delight. Delight expanding bursts into praise, and our hearts overflowing cannot but bubble over with the happy intoxication of luminous truth, and inebr[i]ated with the flow of sweetness cannot refrain from song.[29]

To sing God's praise

As these words of Gilbert just said, the praise of God, when it has really taken root in a heart, spreads out in songs of joy. A Christian worthy of his baptism ought to have a singing soul, enthusiastic about God.

The *Third Sermon on Various Subjects* of **Saint Bernard** is a commentary on the Song of Hezekiah.[30] Bernard proceeds in two waves. A first paragraph looks at the entire canticle; the second and following take up the explication verse by verse.

The father will make your truth known to the sons.

The saint defines three degrees:

Slave   mercenary (or salaried)   son

The son is the one who contemplates, his conduct is irreproachable, his heart is completely devoted to his father, with a disinterested love. He does not try to avoid suffering or to enjoy the recompense for himself: he seeks his father's glory, he praises. That is the beautiful role of praise.

The slave says, "I will go to the gates of hell."

29. Gilbert, Tract 3.1–3; CF 34:24–26.
30. Is 38:10 ff.

The mercenary says, "I will not see the Lord in the land of the living."

The son says, "We will sing psalms every day of our life in the house of the Lord."

Praise is really disinterested love.

The one who is afraid of going to the gates of hell, and the one who wants to see God for his own rest, both seek their own interest. But the one who wants to sing psalms in the house of the Lord:

> Does not fear the perils which attack him,
> nor covets personal gain,
> but without any doubt, he loves the one whom he
> praises every day of his life.

You can see it: that praise comes from love and goes beyond self, it is loving God more than self, it is loving God and no longer self.

For **Bernard**, monastic life is a life of praise, of singing psalms in God's honor.

Geoffroy left his parents. They saw their son leave in sadness to give himself to Clairvaux. Had not this boy confided to one of his friends who remarked on the imprints of sadness: "I know that I will never be happy again in my life." Saint Bernard, alerted, prayed and a miracle occurred: the aspirant to the monastic life found himself suddenly invaded by a marvelous joy, with an intimate assurance that he would never again be unhappy in his life.

Writing to the parents who had been anxious, **Bernard** reassured them, declaring to them that their son was going to the Father, that he was going to joy, expressions which characterized monastic life for him. In the brief letter that he wrote them, he ends by saying:

> He will serve the Lord with joy and gladness, "his song will
> be of the Lord's, for great is the glory of the Lord."[31]

31. Ps 138. Bernard, Epp 112.2; James, 169.

That phrase is saturated with scriptural texts or allusions; therefore it has a rather archaic flavor, but it says that the life of a monk is characterized by singing psalms, whether in the office or during the whole day. It is what **Bernard** calls elsewhere the *jucunda ruminatio psalmodiæ*, the agreeable rumination of the psalms.[32]

In the same sense, **Gilbert** recommended to the nuns:

> For you every day should be solemn, always a new moon, always a sabbath. Therefore let your lips [one could also think here "your heart"] be like a trumpet of beaten silver; a trumpet which summons not to strife but to gladness, celebration, spiritual canticles![33]

---

32. Bernard, PP 2.2.
33. Gilbert, SC 18.2; CF 20:229.

IX   DOING THE WILL OF GOD

Doing God's will instead of ours, or to put it another way to make our will identical to God's will, truly is to pass from self to God. It is to establish ourselves in God, and there for the soul to find its seat, to rest there; it is quite often to renounce our own self-will, to die to self, to the old man. It is HE, God, who counts. All that, as we have already said, represents different aspects of the same reality.

We will look at the following points:

1) Doing the will of God, conforming our will to his
2) The degrees of conformity to the divine will
3) The will itself
4) One spirit with God, one will with God

1) Doing the will of God; conforming our will to his

Baldwin, in his tractate *On the Cenobitic or Common Life,* shows at one point how love renders good the life of those who live either alone or in community. He says:

> If it has not been made good by the charity of God, then it cannot be called a good life; indeed it should not even be [referred to] as life, but rather the image of death. People who love themselves and serve their own desires are dead while they are still alive. . . . But whoever is truly alive gives his consent to the will of God, since life is in his will.[1]

He adds the following, which is quite to the point:

1. Ps 30.

In just the same way, we want others to love us by giving their consent and agreement to our will, and the more they consent, the more we think they love us. Thus, since love loves having things in common, and consent is necessary [for having things in common], it is clear that love always loves consent. If someone gives his con[-]sent, he feels something in common with another.[2]

If we love God, we bring our will into agreement with God's will. Father de Foucauld said it with his fiery heart, his heart madly in love with Jesus:

My God, give me the feeling of your presence in me and around me, and at the same time that fearful love which we experience in the face of the one we love passionately, and which makes us want to do everything that pleases him, and avoid everything that displeases him.[3]

In his *Second Sermon on Diverse Subjects*, **Saint Bernard** recommends with a certain amount of emotion to his monks that they not waste time. The occupation that ought to retain all our attention is the double knowledge of ourselves and of God. To know ourselves, we must be ready to "suffer" and to "act," that is to say to accept everything which comes and to do everything which practically speaking one can do. Then we are, and it is essential to be, people "of ready hearts." In doing the will of God, we are "justified," we are ready for heaven.[4]

Saint Bernard said elsewhere[5] that when you want to sew one belt to another in order to make one belt, it is absolutely necessary that the end of one belt be adjusted to match the end of the other. In the same fashion, it is absolutely necessary that the end of our present life should be in accord with the eternal life that is going to follow immediately after it. We should be preparing for this end of life by all that precedes it, our everyday

2. Baldwin, Tract 15; CF 41:172–173. Fr Thomas adds the hyphen to stress the connection between the Latin *consentire* (to feel with) and the feeling of unity of sentiment in loving.

3. Charles de Foucauld, *Écritures spirituelles*, 50.

4. Bernard, Div 2.

5. Bernard, PP 2.6.

life. We should have a heart which is ready, justified, and by that, conform our will to God's will.

Our will belongs to us, *but we must give it to God*. **Bernard** said it in his *Twenty-Second Sermon on Various Subjects*, the sermon of the "four debts," or to say it another way, the four reasons for our gratitude toward God, four motives for giving ourselves completely to him:

First reason: He has given so much to me:
I ought to give myself to him!

> I have nothing but two little things (*minuta*), or rather two minuscule little things (*imo minutissima*), my body and my soul, or we could even say just one thing, my will. And I am not willing to sacrifice it to the will of him who, so great himself, has heaped with benefits such an insignificant being as myself (*qui* tantus tantillum tantis *beneficiis prævenit*), and who has completely bought me by giving himself completely (*qui* toto *se* totum *me comparavit*)?
>
> Otherwise, if I retain my will for myself, with what face, with what eyes, with what spirit, with what conscience, will I go to take refuge in the depths of the mercy of God?[6]

The other three reasons

Bernard then lists the other three reasons for giving ourselves totally to God. The second (our second debt, our second creditor): our sins which need to be expiated; the third, heaven which awaits us; and the fourth, the fact that God is our creator and we are his creatures. The man of God then poses the question:

> Explain to me then to which of these creditors you plan to give what you owe him? Each of them is so pressing that he might strangle you [a reference to the parable of the insolvent debtor].

Right away he exposes his own personal case. He realizes that he is absolutely incapable of paying God what he owes him. He gives him the little bit that he has, his will:

6. Bernard, Div 22.6.

O Lord! I suffer violence, hear my pleas![7] Lord, I put what
little I have into your hands. Pay all my debtors, rescue me
from their hands, because you are God and not man and
that which is impossible for men is possible for you.[8]

2) The degrees of conformity to the divine will

Dom Chautard invented a scale, running from bored
acceptance to perfect communion with the divine will:

Ægre—unwillingly
Fiat—giving one or more sighs
Amen—it is already a great deal
ita, Pater—Yes, Father!
Libenter!—willingly, cheerfully!
Ecce adsum!—Here I am! Eagerly
Deo gratias!—thankfully
Alleluia!—a kind of enthusiasm

Often we find degrees of acceptance of the divine will among
our Cistercian authors. They loved spiritual journeys, so they
traced spiritual progress this way.

So **Saint Bernard**, in his *Fifth Sermon on Various Subjects*, says
that the first degree of contemplation is to see what God wants,
what pleases him; you then adjust to that will, conform yourself
to it. There is then a passing from ourselves to God: we no longer
consider what the divine will is for us, but what it is in itself.
We pass from ourselves to the Holy Spirit, which is the divine
Will in person. We find again here that passing from ourselves
to God. Here is the text:

The first degree of contemplation, my beloved friends, is
that we ceaselessly should consider what the Lord wants,
what pleases him, what is agreeable to him. And as we all
fall into a multitude of faults, we should humble ourselves
under the powerful hand of the Most High God, and make
every effort to appear pitiable to the eyes of his mercy,

7. Is 38:14–15.
8. Bernard, Div 9.

saying to him: "Heal me, Lord, and I will be healed; save me and I will be saved"[9]; and again: "Lord have pity on me, heal my soul, because I have sinned against you."[10]

Once our heart has purified itself in such thoughts, we no longer find ourselves wrapped in bitterness in our own spirits, but rather in the Spirit of God we have turned with great rejoicing; and we no longer consider what God's will is concerning us, but what it is in itself.

Having thus distinguished these two degrees or ways of looking at the divine will, one as it concerns us, the other as it concerns God himself, Bernard takes up this teaching again, expressing it in a different way:

> Our life, in effect, is completely in his will,[11] so much so that we cannot doubt that nothing can be more useful to us and more advantageous than that which is conformed to his will. But after we have made some progress in the way of these spiritual exercises, taking as guide the Holy Spirit who scrutinizes the depths of God himself, we will think how sweet the Lord is, how good he is in himself.[12]

Another text, even more characteristic of **Saint Bernard**, is worth pointing out. It has been quoted already elsewhere, when it was a matter of showing how our Fathers spoke of the passing from ourselves to God: one degree of perfection is to seek to please God; another, higher, is simply to be content with God: it is he who pleases us. We are talking about the *Hundred Third Sermon on Various Subjects*. At the highest degree, we no longer seek that God should want what we want, but to want what he wants:

> That man has peace in all things, because God pleases him in all things; he has now learned not to bend the will of God to his own, but to bend his own to God's will.[13]

---

9. Jer 17:14.
10. Ps 41.
11. Ps 30.
12. Bernard, Div 5.5.
13. Bernard, Div 103.4.

In **Gilbert's** *Ninth Sermon on the Song*, we find a quite similar teaching. The author has spoken of the stripping off of the old man, of the clothing in the new. Then, he said, one is more held by God than holding him. Then he adds these words from Psalm 73:

> "You have taken hold of my right hand . . .
> and you have guided me with your counsel."

Gilbert speaks then of a will of God which is given to us. God makes us will. It is the taste of God, the experience of God; it is far superior to the will of the man who forces himself to will what God wills:

> "You have guided me with your counsel," that is, with counsel which is from you and follows you, with counsel which attracts rather than is attracted. For at times we strive with great effort to attract even good counsel and we pursue it like a fugitive rather than follow it as a leader. For so the psalmist says: I have longed to desire.[14] Good is that counsel but not yet pleasant (*justa, sed nondum jucunda*), correct but not yet agreeable. "In your counsel you have guided me," in that counsel which depends on the alluring taste of goodness itself and relies, if I may so express it, not so much on sluggish reason as on a holy delight in goodness itself.[15]

God alone, absolutely alone, can act on our will and make it will freely, but infallibly. It is said that one day Saint Joseph Cottolengo, going to visit the teaching religious whom he had established at Turin, was confronted by one of them who was beside herself: she held by the hand a little girl with whom she could do nothing more, because she was so unbearable. The saint leaned down to the ear of the child, saying a few words to her. Miracle! Soon there was a complete conversion; the little girl became a model of wisdom and docility. Extremely surprised, the religious asked, "What did Father say to you?"; she responded, "I did not understand what he said to me; but while he was speaking to me, I felt a great desire to become good." That is what

14. Ps 119.
15. Gilbert, SC 9.3; CF 14:130.

grace can do: it can make you want to do something. Just one more example: the future Father Ginhac, a Jesuit of great sanctity, while he was a young man, had great need of conversion. His sister who was a Carmelite religious prayed ceaselessly for him. He converted himself, or rather Jesus converted him, as though he himself had nothing to do with it. Here is how he told the event to his sister:

> After the big parade which happened at the end of the mission, going along the street, I saw, carried by young people, a stretcher on which lay a big Christ. All at once, it seemed to me that that figure was shining with clarity and that it pierced my heart. I had to lower my eyes, and I felt completely changed inside. I no longer recognized myself. From that time on, I have been disposed to give myself completely to God.
>
> A word of the Father explains perhaps what that look was: "For my vocation, I was drawn along with such a force that the whole universe armed against me would not have shaken me. Under that divine influence, I entered the Company, and, at a certain moment, Our Lord made me understand that he called me to perfection, and that I would arrive there." The Father repeated these last words twice.[16]

Let us come back . . . to our Fathers! Above all we must consult **Baldwin of Ford** here. In his tractate *On the Love of God*, he reviews in a very fine manner the different ways of uniting oneself to the will of God, of wanting what he wants. Rather than reproducing here the text itself, let us express in simpler, clearer terms the degrees which he distinguishes:

1) The sort of will of God which is imposed on me doesn't please me. Knowing that it pleases God doesn't move me. It's only I who count: I know that if I don't obey, I am going to have to pay dearly for it . . .

2) I want what God wants, because God wants it and I love God; therefore I want what he wants, but I do not love the thing which he demands.

16. Fr Calvet, *Vie du Père Ginhac*, 18.

3) I love the thing itself, because he loves it. I love God so much that I love everything he loves.

That is how it is with *love for one's enemies*: there is something God wills, a commandment. I can bend to it grudgingly; I can want to love my enemies because God commands me, but I would very much have preferred that he didn't ask it of me. In the third case, I love to love my enemies, because that pleases God.[17]

3) Self-will

What then is "self-will"? It is going your own way instead of obeying.

Saint Bernard speaks of those whom one must ask, "What do you want me to do for you?", when they ought to be saying with Saint Paul, "What do you want me to do?"

> Today such is the weakness and the malice of many that we are obliged ask them what their will is, and say to them, "What do you want me to do for you?", when they ought to be saying, "Lord, what do you want me to do?"
>
> The ministers and representatives of Christ are required to seek out what these men want people to tell them to do. They do not concern themselves with what their master wants.
>
> The obedience of these monks is not complete, they are not disposed to obey in everything, they do not have any intention of following everywhere the one who did not come to earth to do his own will, but that of the Father. They discern, they decide the things in which they will obey the one who gives them orders, or rather those in which their superior ought to obey their will.
>
> May those who are of this disposition not rest in that state, even if they are supported in it, even if others condescend to their weakness; I swear to you, that they should blush to be treated like little children, if they do not wish to hear addressed to themselves this word: "What must I do for you that I have not already done?"[18]

17. Baldwin, Tract 3; CF 39:97.
18. Bernard, Pl 1.6.

Further, **Saint Bernard** delineates in a very precise sense what he means by "self-will": it is opposed to the "common will." We find this thought especially in two of his sermons for Easter.

In order to buy perfumes, he said in the second, we must pay with money, the coin, the silver of self-will (*nummo propriæ voluntatis*). We do not lose anything, on the contrary we gain in that purchase, because we do nothing but exchange our self-will for common will. And the common will is charity. At bottom, it is always the same teaching: we lose ourselves in order to find ourselves, we die to ourselves in order to find our life again in God:

> Then we buy without giving anything in exchange, for we acquire what we did not have at all, and what we did have, we keep better than it was before.[19]

Bernard here paints a picture of those who are deluded about themselves, and hoodwink others; they pass as true monks, and believe themselves to be so. But no, they do not have that charity which is the common will, they keep their self-will:

> That brother may feign in the eyes of men, and even delude himself, to the point of believing it, so long as he allows himself to be led by his own self love or by hate, or is moved by compassion or by the zeal for justice. But it is easy to see how distant the acts of charity are from those of self-will.[20]

In his *Third Sermon for Easter*, the saint defines with even more precision that self-will which he calls a "leprosy of the heart."

> By self-will I mean that which is not in common with God nor with men, but is truly "self," which happens when we want what we want neither for the glory of God, nor for the good of our neighbor, but for our own personal satisfaction.

19. Bernard, Pasc 2.8.
20. Bernard, Pasc 2.8.

It is diametrically opposed to charity, which is nothing else
but God. In effect it lifts up enmities with God, and declares
a merciless war against him. Because what is it that God
detests and punishes, if not self-will? If self-will ceased to
exist, there would be no more hell! What prey would its fire
devour, if not self-will?[21]

The Lord has recommended to the one who wants to be on
the roof (the terrace) of his house, in the moment of the "great
tribulation," not to redescend (by the interior stairway) inside the
house, "to retrieve anything." **John of Ford** interprets this phrase
freely; he thinks that for the monk, his self-will is "something
which he must not take up again. By his monastic profession,
he has abandoned it, he has climbed up to the roof"—precisely
his monastic profession. He should not go back down into his
house to take up his self-will again. It sticks to the skin, and it
tries to come back when one is rid of it. It is a troublemaker, not
only for the soul that keeps it, but for the community.

There is a real danger, after having given yourself completely
to God with a heartfelt obedience, of taking back that gift. **Isaac**,
in his *Third Sermon for the Assumption*, says it as tersely as anyone
could. It is a very pretty sermon, in which he distinguishes three
steps in the ascent toward God, following the words of a verse
of Psalm 73:

> You have held out to me your right hand: it is the
>   beginning.
> And you have led me in your will: it is all of life.
> And in your justice you have welcomed me: it is the end.

All your life, to be led in the will of God. Upon arriving in
Heaven, the Holy Virgin, on the day of her Assumption, said to
God, "You have led me in your will."

> She said in *your* and not in *my*; Mary was not led in her will.
> Furthermore, in the gospel, the apostles learned to pray to
> the Father saying, "*Your* will be done."

Having commented on the psalm verse, applying it to the
Virgin Mary, Isaac dreams of the monks who have taken back

21. Bernard, Pasc 3.3.

their self-will, who follow it, who do whatever comes into their heads, and he tells them off:

> I ask myself how we can find such stupidity among certain people, in particular among those who have abdicated their self-will, promising to obey men; we see them battling every day to do their own will. They murmur against God on numerous occasions and resist his plans, by revolting against the authority which stems from him, intending to be their own masters. "It's in such and such a way, they say, that we will act; now this, now that." Still greater folly: they want to teach and organize everything according to their own will: "It's in such and such a way they say that they ought to act." And if someone steps over the line, there they are murmuring, denigrating, judging, and condemning.[22]

Let us retain this phrase so well coined, **Isaac**'s again, in his *Second Sermon for Saint John the Baptist*. It is a question of the voice of the Spouse, that of Christ through the voice of our superiors: be careful not to rejoice only when they command what pleases us:

> Many rejoice to hear a lot of words, but not because of the voice of the Spouse. Many obey numerous orders that they receive but not because of the voice of the Spouse. When they hear what pleases their will, they rejoice on account of themselves, and in that they have already received their recompense. When someone commands them to do what they want, they obey willingly, but following their own desires. They have nothing to wait for from the Spouse; that which is not done for him will not receive any recompense.
>
> Every "ecclesiastical" ordinance [all authority emanating from the church] is the voice of the Spouse. Whoever judges it or despises it cannot be the friend of the Spouse. Every word, every command that comes from your superiors is the voice of the Spouse. Whoever despises or neglects them, throws himself into enmity [against the Spouse]. In any case, if he only executes the command with disgust, with

22. Isaac, 3 Asspt; PL 194:1871B–C; PC 28:31.

bitterness of heart and murmuring of the mouth, he has not yet arrived at friendship.

The Spouse is the Word of God. Every happening is his voice. Everything that happens in time exists from all eternity in the Word of God. Everything happens as the Word causes or permits it to happen, and nothing happens without his will: every *outside* event is the voice of the Word. The person who *on the inside* loves everything which has been decided cannot murmur about what happens. Everything comes from the will of a good God, and is accomplished perfectly according to his ways, and the good ought therefore to love him.

The following lines show us how this accomplishment of the divine will comes to be a true communion with God, forgetfulness of self, and disinterested love.

The perfection of every religious life and of all obedience is to love what God loves, because God loves it; to hate what God hates, because God hates it; to want what God wants, because God wants it; not to want what God doesn't want, because God doesn't want it.

Everything we apprehend from outside [ourselves] shows us the will of God, as if he were speaking to us. If we want to be the Spouse's friends, even if certain events cause us pain, we rejoice nevertheless, because of the voice that shows us the will of the Spouse.[23]

This text leads us completely naturally to the next point.

4) One spirit together with God, one will together with God

Christ Jesus, in his human nature, has a human will and human action. Completely playing the part of his condition as a man, he has wanted on earth completely to submit his will to that of his Father. In John chapter 5, he is presented, or presents himself to us, as doing nothing without his Father, not having thoughts, words, or wishes except what he sees the Father doing. It is a perfect fidelity to communicate always to everyone what his Father thinks, loves, and wants.

23. Isaac, 2 Nat JB, PL 194:1851C–D.

Such is our model. Not for nothing are we children in the Son; not for nothing are we animated by the same Spirit of Jesus; he pushes us to cry out "Abba! Father!"; he pushes us to have only one spirit with him. We can so thoroughly conform our wills to God's (with his grace) that they merge completely with his.

Baldwin of Ford in his tractate *On the Cenobitic or Common Life* speaks of this perfect accord which achieves unity.

> If, then, the charity of God which is in us can be so much in accord with the charity with which God loves us that it loves that which he himself loves, if it always pursues the better things in its zeal for perfection and is always careful to avoid even the lighter sins, if it regards as contemptible what God also wants regarded as contemptible, then this charity of God brings about in us unity of spirit, and as the only-begotten Son of God lives with God the Father in the unity of the Holy Spirit (for there is but one Spirit of the Father and the Son), so we too, as adopted sons, live under God the Father in the unity of the Holy Spirit, and it is in this [Spirit] that we cry, "Abba, Father". . . . Our cry, therefore, certainly comes from far away, but yet, in a certain way, there is a similarity.[24]

William of Saint-Thierry has a magnificent teaching on this subject. It is a doctrine, one might even say a theory. Reflecting to begin with on the words of Scripture, the writings of Saint John and Saint Paul in particular, reflecting also on his personal experience, on what he was able to understand from spiritual men like his friend Saint Bernard about their own experiences, he has elaborated a doctrine, and the **unity of spirit** is the summit of it. The Holy Spirit can so take hold of a soul, of a human will, of the love of a person, that what the spirit does in the breast of the Trinity, what he is, the Unity of the Father and the Son, he is in an analogous way between the soul and God. He becomes their kiss, their communion, their unity. At a certain point, in an intense moment of grace, the soul is not able to want anything except what God wants.

---

24. Baldwin, Tract 15; CF 41:175–176.

That teaching is not merely theoretical, it comes from lived experience, and it is achieved in life, in the daily round: to the extent that a person receives this influx of graces, he or she will no longer want to do anything but the will of God, to have with him a single willing and a single not-willing; it is a loving and defect-free observance of the commandments. Let us cite a few texts:

> And when your love, that is, the love of the Father for the Son and the love of the Son for the Father—the Holy Spirit, when he dwells in us, he is to you that which he is—love. And he turns toward himself and hallows all the "captives of Sion,"[25] that is to say, all the affections of the soul. And when he does all that, we love you, or you love yourself in us, we affectively and you effectively, making us one in you, through your own unity, through your Holy Spirit whom you have given us. So it comes to this: that as for the Father to know the Son is nothing else but to be what the Son is, and for the Son to know the Father is simply to be what the Father is (whence comes the Gospel saying: "No one knows the Father save the Son, and no one knows the Son except the Father"), and as for the Holy Spirit to know and understand the Father and the Son is simply to be what the Father and the Son are, so is it with us. We were created in your image. Through Adam we have grown old in unlikeness; but now through Christ we are being renewed in that image day by day. So for us who love God, I tell you, to love and fear God is nothing other than to be of one spirit with him. For to fear God and keep his commandment, that is the whole of man.[26]

We come back to present a passage from the *Commentary on the Song* which also goes from the most sublime experience to humble daily life.

> Blessed is she [the soul] whose conscience, come weal come woe in this world, draws from heaven the pattern it should use and the manner of its life. Wherever she turns, from your

25. Ps 126.
26. Qo 12:13. William, Contemp 17; CF 3:58.

countenance, O God, comes forth her judgment, that she may ever be united to you by likeness in willing the same thing; for she withdraws not from you but by unlikeness in willing. Therefore whoever is a Bride has but one desire, one aspiration—namely that her face may continually be joined to your Face in the kiss of charity, that is, that she may become one spirit with you through unity of will with you; that the form of her life may be ardently impressed to the form of your love, by the ardor of great love; or should the material prove unyielding, that it may be broken and set in order by the force of discipline.

But after this has been consummated, the light of your countenance, O Lord, is signed upon your Bride, your love, your beautiful one, and its gladness is set in order in her devout soul, where now all duly proceeds according to the order of charity. Sleeping and taking her rest in the selfsame peace, she rejoices in the Bridegroom's embrace and says: "His left hand is under my head, and his right hand shall embrace me."[27]

This embrace extends to man, but it surpasses man. For this embrace is the Holy Spirit. He is the Communion, the Charity, the Friendship, the Embrace of the Father and of the Son of God; and he himself is all these things in the love of Bridegroom and Bride. But on the one hand stands the majesty of consubstantial Nature; on the other, the gift of grace. On the one hand, dignity; on the other, condescension (*dignitas . . . dignatio*). Nevertheless it is the same, absolutely the same Spirit.[28]

Nevertheless by far the most important text is found in the *Letter to the Brothers of Mont-Dieu*, the famous *Golden Epistle*:

But "unity of spirit" with God for the man who has his heart raised on high is the term of the will's progress toward God. No longer does it merely desire what God desires, not only does it love him, but it is perfect in its love, so that it can will only what God wills.

Now to will what God wills is already to be like God, to be able to will only what God wills is already to be what God

27. Sg 8:3.
28. William, Cant 131–132; CF 6:105–106.

is; for him to will and to be are the same thing. Therefore
it is well said that we shall see him fully as he is when we
are like him, that is when we are what he is. For those who
have been enabled to become sons of God have been able
to become not indeed God, but what God is . . .

William insists on this resemblance of man to God, a
resemblance that has acquired an exceptional dimension. After
having spoken of the resemblance which is written in human
nature itself, then of the resemblance of the virtues, he comes to
that marvelous resemblance which is unity of spirit, where the
will is as though captivated, made captive, incapable of being
able to act in contradiction to God.

> This likeness . . . is so close in its resemblance that it is
> styled not merely a likeness but unity of spirit. It makes
> man one with God, one spirit, not only with the unity which
> comes of willing the same thing but with a greater fullness
> of virtue, as has been said: the inability to will anything
> else.
>
> It is called unity of spirit not only because the Holy Spirit
> brings it about or inclines a man's spirit to it, but because it
> is the Holy Spirit himself, the God who is Charity. He who
> is the Love of Father and Son, their Unity, Sweetness, Good,
> Kiss, Embrace and whatever else they can have in common
> in that supreme unity of truth and truth of unity, becomes
> for man in regard to God in the manner appropriate to him
> what he is for the Son in regard to the Father or for the
> Father in regard to the Son through unity of substance. The
> soul in its happiness finds itself standing midway in the
> Embrace and Kiss of Father and Son. In a manner which
> exceeds description and thought, the man of God is found
> worthy to become not God but what God is, that is to say
> man becomes through grace what God is by nature.[29]

29. William, Ep frat II.15, 16; CF 12:95–96.

X BELIEVING IN THE LOVE OF GOD

In order to pass from self to God, which is the theme of this retreat, it is necessary, with the grace of God, **to forget yourself**, which requires energy and perseverance. You must really want it. It is also necessary **to be very small**, to count only on grace to forget yourself in this way and to pass from self to God. These two points are not at all contradictory. It is also necessary **to believe in the love of God**.

Permit me, in this last chapter, this last lesson if you wish, to share a few things, to give you something from my soul.

In my understanding, these three efforts which have God as their goal, to forget yourself, to be small, to believe in His love, are closely linked, interwoven with each other, and they govern one's entire spiritual life. This conviction did not occur to me as a result of study and reflection, but spontaneously out of nowhere, although reflection and study have been able to reinforce it strongly. The realization was a grace, let me tell you, which has marked my life. After that memorable retreat in 1930, given by Father Godefroid (who later became Dom Godefroid, abbot of Cîteaux), it emerged forcefully and yet without effort: at first *I do not wish to occupy myself with anything but God*, not with myself; I do not want to know if I am good or bad, well-esteemed or not, but I want only to know God. He is always the same, always so good, independently of me: "For your part, my God, you are good." Then the second light, the second resolution, the second conviction to pass frequently in my heart: *I come to you, my God, as a little child.* By my own efforts, I could not get there. Whatever I do myself is laughable. But you will cause the impossible to happen, namely to make me arrive at union with you, at sanctity. Finally *to believe in love*. I believe in your love for me. I am loved by my Father in heaven, by Jesus, by the Holy Virgin. For me, even just for me, Jesus would do it all over again. Oh! What joy! Joy!

With the perspective of many years, it is still the same conviction, but reinforced. Everything is there: forgetting oneself, behaving like a small child with God, believing in his love. I would add this: I do not dare say that I forget myself more than at the beginning of my religious life, I just don't know anything about that; nor that I am now smaller before God; but as for what it is to believe in the love of God, oh, that yes, I believe it more, and I have good reason to do so!

Let's look at three points:

> God loves us, God loves me
> How to believe in that love
> Where that leads us

1) God loves us

You know what it is to be loved. To be loved is to have gained a heart. If someone loves you, it's because he finds you "lovable," and it is sweet to know yourself lovable in the eyes and heart of someone else. Love is more than simply wishing someone well or doing nice things for them. I can wish someone well without being in love with him. To say that God loves us is not just to notice that he has given us blessings, but that he is truly in love with us. Nevertheless when someone pays with himself, when he sacrifices himself for someone, it is the undeniable proof that he loves the other person, and there is no greater love than to give your life for those you love.

Who then could examine the very heart of God to judge the measure of his love! You have to have in yourself the Holy Spirit who discerns the secrets of God to know something about it. And Jesus has revealed the love of the Father for us, to the degree that it is understandable by us.

There are two marvels before which Saint John exclaims in surprise, in joy, in abandon. Two great manifestations of the love of the Father before which he goes into ecstasy! "For God so loved the world that he gave his only-begotten Son."[1] First, the Incarnation, the gift of his Son coming to us with a humanity like ours. Seeing Jesus is to see the Father; it is to find the heart of the Father in the heart of Jesus, so good and so loving. And that Incarnation is completely aimed at the Redemption, the cross, the Passion, the great follies of God's love. John's other joyous exclamation sprang out when considering our divine sonship: "See what love the Father had that we are called his children, and so we are!"[2] We must read and meditate slowly on the admirable lines in which Father Spicq[3] comments on this phrase of St. John, then close our eyes and keep silence to allow the idea to penetrate: the Father loves me, I am his child! To be able to say to God, "Abba! Daddy!" And it is the Holy Spirit, the Spirit of Jesus who cries out this word in my heart!

We can say, "The Father has given me everything, his Son, his Spirit; not only given his Son, but allowed me to be melted together with his Son, to say with him, 'Father, daddy!' He has given me everything with Jesus, the Holy Virgin and all the treasure of grace, the sacraments, supernatural life, and later heaven . . . "

Allow me to point out now the qualities, the characteristics of this love. Here are at least some of them:

It is a personal love for each one of us

Saint Paul rightly says, "He has loved *me* and has given himself up for *me*."[4] Each of us can say, "He thought personally of me when he was given up to go to death; he thought of me all during his life, and now Jesus still loves me all the time." To be loved as part of a group, together with others, is a great deal less touching than to be loved personally. The Father loves me, myself; he sees in me his own child.

1. Jn 3:16.
2. 1 Jn 3:1.
3. Ceslas Spicq, *Agapé dans le Nouveau Testament: analyse des textes* (Paris: J. Gabalda, 1958–1959) III:252–255; 324–326.
4. Gal 2:20.

Here is what we read in the writings of Saint Pierre-Julien Eymard:

> What makes the love of God stronger and more powerful is that it is personal, limited to each one of us, as though we were alone in the world. A person completely penetrated by the divine truth that God loves him personally, that it is for love for him alone that he has created the world and its marvels . . . , that person ought to explode with love, live with love, be consumed by love.[5]

William of Saint-Thierry already wrote in his *Exposition on the Song*:

> Christ the Bridegroom offered to his Bride the Church, so to speak, a kiss from heaven, when the Word made flesh drew so near to her that he wedded her to himself; and so wedded her that he united her to himself, in order that God might become man, and man might become God. He also offers this same kiss to the faithful soul, his Bride, and imprints it upon her, when from the remembrance of the benefits common to all men, he gives her her own special and personal joy and pours forth within her the grace of his love, drawing her spirit to himself and infusing into her his spirit, that both may be one spirit.[6]

In the same work, William has slipped in a few lines that at first sight can appear mysterious, but that have a very profound meaning and can enchant us:

> That comes to pass in the lover which you once said of such a one, "He who loves me will be loved by my Father, and I will love him and manifest myself to him."[7] For *when one day the lover, by loving thus, is somewhat more deserving of a loftier grace, he begins indeed to be loved (incipit diligens etiam diligi).*[8]

Obviously it is God who begins to love first, but as the words of the evangelist cited here say, we respond to the prevenient

---

5. Pierre-Julien Eymard, *La divine Eucharistie* II:201.
6. William, Cant 30; CF 6:25–26.
7. Jn 14:21.
8. William, Cant 57; CF 6:46. Emphasis added by Fr Thomas.

love of God by loving; then one day, *God lets us feel that we are loved*, and that changes our whole life: it is a revelation of Jesus to the soul.

It is a grace to claim the love that God has for us; **Saint Bernard** had it, when he wrote:

> How wonderful your love for me, my God, my love! How wonderful your love for me[!][9]

God provokes our love by loving us. It is by showing us that he loves us personally that he makes us decide to come out of ourselves and pass into him through love, to dwell in him, to leave ourselves in order to live in him through a loving recollection.

It is a first love

"God loved us first," says Saint John again.[10] And that is not like the priority of human loves. When two people love each other, we can say, "There is one of the two who began to love," she first found the other lovable. In God, the priority of loving is a completely different thing. "God loves me," each of us can say. Did he find me lovable? Yes, certainly. But that lovableness is not something that was already there, that God found and that went to his heart. His heart is certainly touched, he loves me, but that love is inexplicable. Why does he love me, why do I please him? It is because he wanted it that way; he is the one who has made it so that I am attractive to him, he is the one who has given me the lovableness which draws him. **Saint Bernard** writes:

> "O Lord, what is man that thou shouldst notice him, or the son of man that thou shouldst give heed to him?" Already, O loving Father, that most vile worm, worthy of everlasting hatred, is confident that it is loved because it feels that it loves (*confidit amari quoniam se sentit amare*): or rather because it divines that it is loved, it is ashamed not to love in return.[11]

9. Bernard, SC 17.7; CF 4:131.
10. 1 Jn 4:10.
11. Bernard, Epp 109.7 (Cist ed 107.7); James 162.

In his *Fifth Sermon for Lent*, **Guerric** says some very beautiful things while commenting on the parable of the prodigal son. The father, image of the heavenly Father, hurries even faster to forgive his son than the son does to receive pardon. It is the tenderness of God who wants to make us understand that God loves us more than we love ourselves. Here is the way Guerric explains the phrase in the parable, "He threw himself on his neck and kissed him":

> When he showed him such affection, what was he looking for in that embrace, in those kisses, if not to make his son come into himself, and to go into his son himself, if not to give his own spirit to his son? He wanted by attaching himself to him that he should become one spirit with him, just as by attaching himself to prostitutes he became one body with them. It would have been too little for sovereign Mercy merely not to withhold the depth of his mercy from the miserable; he went so far as to draw them, to build them into his members. Mercy could not unite us more closely to itself, it could not have a more intimate bond than in incorporating us into itself, in uniting us, as much by the effect of its love as by that of its ineffable power, not only to the body which it had assumed, but even to his own spirit.[12]

Love without cost, disinterested

In the end, frankly, God does not need us, and he does not need our love. It is stupefying to consider God's love from that angle. I remember that philosophy teaches us that God's love in creation is the purest, the most disinterested there is, because if God cannot have anything but his glory as the goal of everything that he makes, the beneficiary of creation—*finis cui*, as we say in scholarly terms—, is really mankind and not God himself! What do we make then of the Incarnation and the Passion? More than once **Bernard** returns to this thought which struck him. Let's cite just one example:

12. Guerric, Quad 5; SCh 202:31. Fr Thomas cites as 2.

It was less easy to remake me than to make me. It is written
not only about me but of every created being; "He spoke
and they were made."[13] But he who made me by a single
word, in remaking me had to speak many words, work
miracles, suffer hardships, and not only hardships but even
unjust treatment. "What shall I render to the Lord for all
that he has given me?" In his first work he gave me myself;
in his second work he gave me himself; when he gave me
himself, he gave me back myself.[14]

Guerric has a real talent, a "charism" for representing the
excessive love of God. So it is in the *First Sermon for Palm Sunday*.
We see all the steps of creation, the fall, and the raising up of
mankind unfurled there. Mankind, created to serve God, who
revolts crying out "I will not serve!" Christ's attitude is the polar
opposite of that of sinful mankind: he made himself man, he took
the form of a servant, of a slave. That was not enough: he made
himself the servant, the slave of his slave:

He also served his own slave as more than a slave.

Here is the dialogue that occurred between God and man:

"I will not serve," man says to his Creator.
"Then I will serve you," his Creator says to man. "You sit
down, I will minister, I will wash your feet. You rest; I will
bear your weariness, your infirmities. *Use me as you like in
all your need*, not only as your slave but also as your beast of
burden and as your property. If you are tired or burdened
I will carry both you and your burden, so that I may be the
first to keep my own law, 'Bear one another's burdens,' we
read, 'and so you will fulfill the law of Christ.' If you are
hungry or thirsty . . . I am ready to be slaughtered that
you may eat my flesh and drink my blood. . . . If you are
led into captivity or sold, here I am, sell me and redeem
yourself at my cost . . . . If you are ill and afraid to die I
will die for you . . . ."[15]

13. Ps 148.
14. Bernard, Dil V.15; CF 13B:18.
15. Guerric, Palm 1.1; CF 32:55–56.

Guerric congratulates this "good servant" who was Christ and he gives in more detail the marvelous aspects of his service:

> Well done, good and faithful servant. You have served indeed, you have served with all loyalty and trustworthiness, you have served with all patience and endurance . . .

In contrast, there is the scene of the proud man who refused to serve, who was not able to be led to be humble except by seeing his Lord and master submitting himself to such a service, to such humiliations.

The last part of the sermon is the most beautiful. It is the dénouement. Man is at last conquered by so much love. Guerric, moved, imagines himself in the scene:

> Indeed you have toiled hard, my Lord, in serving me. It were only just and fair that at least for the future you should rest and your slave, if only because it is his turn, should serve you. . . . [Y]ou have . . . overcom[e] evil with good, . . . overwhelming ingratitude with benefits. . . . You have conquered, Lord, you have conquered the rebel; behold I surrender to your bonds, I put my neck under your yoke. Only deign to let me serve you, suffer me to toil for you.[16]

Is a text of that sort not a provocation to love? It invites us to give ourselves completely. What wouldn't we do for someone by whom we know ourselves profoundly loved? We can read attentively the *Second Sermon for Lent* or the *First Sermon for Pentecost*, where we find beautiful thoughts presented in such a way as to make us reflect on and touch them. Isn't the following phrase taken from the latter sermon a flame of fire:

> O God, if I may be allowed to speak thus, you lavish yourself on man far beyond his dreams.[17]

In his treatise *On Contemplating God*, we find **William** also has this lovely word for us about what Christ accomplished in his supremely disinterested love for us:

16. Guerric, Palm 1.3; CF 32:57–58.
17. Guerric, Pent 1.1; CF 32:109.

He said to us: "I love you so that you will love me!"[18]

or to put it another way, I love you so that, responding to my love, you may find joy. **William** said this still more explicitly in his treatise *On the Sacrament of the Altar*:

> Everything that our Redeemer did during his mortal life had as its goal provoking our love. Not because he had need of it personally, he had only to bless us; but having received the mission of making us happy, he could not do it unless we loved him.[19]

All these texts have said to us over and over again: God loves us, God loves me. We must be silent, draw back, and wonder at this. After which, we say to ourselves: we must believe in the love of God, "live in his love," and give ourselves unfailingly to love, actually to love. Let us ask, according to what has been proclaimed, how to believe practically in love.

2) How to believe practically in love

In a general manner, we must try to become accustomed *to see the love of God everywhere*. It is not our thought or imagination which believes it, it is our faith which discovers it. Our faith, as **Saint Bernard** put it, is *oculata*,[20] it has eyes, and "the eyes of a lynx"[21]; it knows how to discover things that are hidden from simple "human" eyes, such as that everything that happens comes from the love of God, or at least is controlled by his love. I am sure I am not deceiving myself in saying about whatever happens to me: "God knows everything, he can do everything and he loves me; this fits into his loving plan for me."

Believe in the love and tenderness of God through everything, and what tenderness! The holy Curé of Ars said:

---

18. William, Contemp 12; CF 3:167–178, paraphrased.
19. William, Sac altar V; PL 180:351C.
20. Bernard, Asc 6.15.
21. Bernard, Epi 2.4.

God holds the interior man as a mother holds the head of her child in her hands in order to cover it with kisses and caresses.[22]

Closer to us, Pius XII, in his encyclical *Mystici corporis*:

> In the manger, on the cross, in the eternal bosom of the Father, Christ knows and holds united all the members of his Church in a fashion infinitely more clear and more loving than a mother does with her infant hugged to her breast, and than each of us knows and loves himself.[23]

Believe in the love and the divine tenderness; Father Auguste Valensin believed in it. A passage from his *Meditation on Death* has already been cited; here is another from that same meditation:

> Imagine that I am going to find Tenderness: I will go to him and say, "I do not think of myself as worth anything, except for having believed in your goodness." There is in effect my power, all my power, my only power; if that were to leave me, if that confidence in love deserted me, everything would be finished, because I have not the feeling of being worth anything supernaturally; and if it is necessary to be worthy of happiness to have it, it is in order to renounce it. But the longer I live, the more I see that I am right to perceive my Father as infinite indulgence . . . . I am not afraid of God, but it is less because I love him than because I know myself loved by him.

The section following this admirable meditation must be quoted here, because it shows what part this man must play, or any man who wants to follow the same road of confidence, of total faith in the tenderness of God: *he must accept that love*:

> And I do not find a need to ask why my Father loves me or what he loves in me. I would be very embarrassed to respond. He loves me because he is Love, and it is enough that *I accept being loved by him* in order to be loved in fact. But *it is necessary that I make that personal act of accepting*. That

---

22. Text cited in Curé d'Ars, *Vie spirituelle*, t. XC, 44.
23. Text cited in Curé d'Ars, *Vie spirituelle*, t. XC, 44.

is the dignity, even the beauty of the Love which wishes it. Love does not impose itself, it offers itself. O my God, thank you for loving me! And it is not I who would cry out to you that I am unworthy. In any case to love me myself, just as I am, that is worthy of you, worthy of essential Love, worthy of love which is in its essence freely given.[24]

Believe in love. Like the small child (we see that we go back to spiritual infancy, the "being small" of our retreat, because everything is linked together), to be the small child who is not aware of his unworthiness, but of his lack of ability, that he always needs someone to help him, who finds it normal that people love him, that he blooms in affection, in the love in which his life is bathed.

Believe in love. We must try to realize what God's love for us is like, for us personally, we must believe he loves us. And not as though it were just a habit, usual, banal, but in a fresh way, completely new, always rejuvenated.

Having been for a long time the chaplain of the nuns of Chambarand, I knew the families well, especially those of the religious whom I had seen enter the monastery. I knew the names of their brothers and sisters, sometimes those of their nephews or nieces. One day the sister of a religious arrived with her whole little band. Looking at them each in turn, I pronounced the names in order of age: Jean-Paul, Odile, Agnes, but I could not remember the name of the last one, as tall as three apples.[25] I stooped down (and I had to stoop a long way!) and I said to him, "What is your name?" He answered something, but I did not understand. Then the mother who had understood said, "He answered, 'Pierre-Marie-dear'; his name is Pierre-Marie, but he has heard himself called 'dear' so often that he thinks it's part of his name!" Bravo! That's how we must act with God, with Jesus: he says our name and adds "dear," Colette dear, Robert dear, whoever you are. To know yourself loved, dear: an act of faith. *Believe in love.*

24. Auguste Valensin, *La joie dans la foi.* (Paris: Éditions Montaigne, 1954) 106.
25. "as tall as three apples" is a literal translation; we might say, "knee-high to a grasshopper."

In the monastery of Sept-Fons, I had a holy great-uncle, a real saint, who was Dom Chautard's prior for a good thirty years. I think that after God and the Holy Virgin, it's to him that I owe my vocation. He said to me one day, while speaking of what theology terms "conservation," to express the continuation of the creative act which keeps us in existence, "It's as if, at every instant, God says to us: 'I create you, I create you; I will you to be, I will you to be; *I love you, I love you.*'"

Monsignor Gonon, bishop of Moulins, gave our annual retreat in 1928. He developed the theme: "Coming from God to us, there is nothing but love; coming from us to God, there ought to be nothing but love." Walking in the woods, I could say to myself that it is for me, through love for me, that he has made all these trees grow, he knew that one day I would bless him for these created things which give me joy. Finding some salad on my plate some evening, I could say to myself that this little leaf which would have been able to keep on growing is not, because he destined it for me, etc. That may seem naiveté, but I do not believe it is. It is lifting the soul toward God, it is faith, overflowing love, not to imagine yet again, but truly to discover, to unearth the love of God for each one of us, *in everything we see or encounter.* That is the truth.

That is how, in practice, we believe in the love of God.

One last word, a golden phrase from **Saint Bernard**:

Easily they love more who realize they are loved more.[26]

3) Where does this faith in the love of God lead us?

I answer with a single idea: *to loving.* How could you expect that we will not set ourselves to loving God with all our heart when we know ourselves profoundly, tenderly loved by him, we know that he gives us his love, and that he wants us to welcome him with all our might?

Letting ourselves be loved is not so easy. It demands self-forgetfulness, getting beyond self, but when we have risen above

26. Bernard, Dil III.7; CF 13B:9.

ourselves, then we love. "There is nothing but loving and letting oneself be loved," said Elizabeth of the Trinity, "and that all the time." Then, in the measure in which we let ourselves be loved because we believe in love, we love in return.

In the first pages of his book *Dieu nous aime* (*God loves us*), Dom Godefroid Bélorgey wrote,

> It ought to be easy for us to love God: love is an aspiration so strongly engraved in the most intimate part of our nature! And nevertheless, if we examine only our personal response, without looking around us, what can we say? Why then do we not love God, or love him so little? Let us state it plainly: it is because we do not believe efficaciously enough in his love for us. The saints themselves have believed in this love, and that is why they responded with all their might.[27]

Nothing can make us love someone like knowing ourselves truly, faithfully, tenderly loved by him or her. That has been true for mankind in all times, and what **William** says in his *On Contemplating God* is true for us today, as it was true for the people in the twelfth century. After celebrating the love of the Father for us, manifested in the Incarnation, he writes:

> How much and in what sort of way you loved us, in that you spared not your own Son, but delivered him up for us all. Yes, and he himself loved us and gave himself for us.

He adds this fine observation:

> For you, O God, our souls' Creator, knew that this affection cannot be forced in the souls of the sons of men, but *has to be evoked.* . . . You "first loved us"; and you love all your lovers first.[28]

We find many texts and discussions of God's love in **Gilbert of Hoyland**'s writing, among others this thought, speaking of Jesus:

> He loves, and that makes him lovable.

27. Godefroid Bélorgey, *Dieu nous aime* (Paris, 1949) 13.
28. William, Contemp 10; CF 3:52, 53. Fr Thomas cites as Contemp 13.

He abases himself, and his abasements are the manifest proofs of his goodness:

> The more commonplace the things he did for me, the greater evidence he gave me of his goodness,[29]

which makes us think of the famous text of **Saint Bernard**:

> The more he is despised for me, the dearer he becomes to me.[30]

Addressing some nuns, **Gilbert** told them that they could never love Jesus as much as he deserved:

> Your desires for Christ, holy women, burn with a restless and passionate affection, but he is much more lovable than he is loved by you.[31]

From an earlier sermon, we can still extract these lines which manifest a great love, fruit of faith in an incommensurable love; the love of the soul which responds as it can, and that is always too little, to the love of God for it, manifested in Christ Jesus:

> "I found him," she says, "I found him," though previously he sought and found me like a stray sheep, like a lost coin, and in his mercy anticipated me.
> He forestalled me, I say, in finding me when I was lost. He anticipated me, though I deserved nothing. He found me astray, he anticipated me in my despair. He found me in my unlikeness, he anticipated me in my diffidence. He found me by pointing out my state to me, he anticipated me by recalling me to his own. He found me wandering in a labyrinth, he anticipated me with gifts when I was devoid of grace. He found me not that I might choose him but that he might choose me. He anticipated me that he might love me before I loved him.

---

29. Gilbert, SC 2.7; CF 14:62. A translation of Fr Thomas's French makes the connection with the next quotation clearer: "The more he was humbled for me, the more he gave me astonishing proofs of his goodness."

30. Bernard, Epi 1.2.

31. Gilbert, SC 19.2; CF 20:240.

> In this way, then, chosen and loved, sought and acquired,
> found and anticipated, how should I not love and seek him
> with an effort according to my strength and with affection
> beyond my strength? I will seek him until gaining my desire
> I may utter my cry of happiness: "I have found him whom
> my soul loves."[32]

It is still that incomprehensible love, absolutely free, that God has for man, manifested in Jesus' coming into the world and in his Passion; it is that love which will always trigger a response of love on the part of the person. Let us bring in a text of **John of Ford**. In his *Thirteenth Sermon on the Song*, he speaks of what we might call "the unfurling of the love of God." He shows how the love of God for the Church is incomparably more beautiful than that of the Church for God. He enumerates the four qualities of the love of God:

—come from such a Majesty
—eternal
—freely given
—immense.

In response to that love which comes from such a Majesty, the Spouse can offer nothing. Nevertheless, she gives what she can, and that is enough for God:

> You are bound to respond to this love
> with all your strength.
> Be careful how you make response!
> The one who loves you
> is exceedingly great,
> and you, utterly unworthy of being loved,
> are quite incapable of returning a love
> commensurate with so high an honor (*rependere vicem*).
> Yet render what little you have,
> render completely all you can do and all you are,
> and that will content him.

---

32. Sg 8:8. Gilbert, SC 8.8; CF 14:124–125.

He does not seek your love
so as to be enriched by you.
Indeed, compared to his love,
yours is a drop in a bucket![33]
Even if it were perhaps a river,
it still holds that "all the rivers flow into the sea, and the sea is not
made greater!"[34]

Here now are John's reflections on the immensity of divine love manifested in the Incarnation, vehement stimulus to the loving response:

Listen to how greatly you are loved:
"God so loved the world
as to give his Only-begotten Son,"[35]
How strongly this incites us to love!
On this errand God has sent
the one and only Son of his love,
consubstantial with himself,
to reveal his love towards us
and incline us to accept it.

. . .

Go forth to meet him,
all you who feel within yourselves
the stirring of holy love!

. . .

Bless in your heart the blessed one
who comes in the name of the Lord,
and bless him who sent him!
For from the goodness of his heart
and the depths of his love,
the Father has uttered a good Word,
and the most certain proof (*exhibitio certissima*)
of his great love is the sending forth of his Only-begotten Son.[36]

33. Is 40:15.
34. Qo 1:7.
35. Jn 3:16.
36. John, SC 13.6; CF 29:241–243.

CONCLUSION

We now come to the end of this retreat, which had as its theme passing from self to God. This title which seemed so simple was found to cover many subjects: Forgetting yourself, turning away from yourself, dying to yourself, being small, losing yourself, abandoning your self-will, and those negative things were aimed at the positive: to find yourself in God, to become one with him, to become Jesus, to become godlike, to be only one spirit, one will with God.

All that is an ideal which will never be perfectly realized here below, but which is a light, a force, toward which, supported by the grace of God, we ought to head generously. Then we will find joy and astonishment; like Gilbert, we will be able to say, "I have found God."

Let us end with a page from Saint Bernard where he finds all these subjects as if by magic, this multiplicity that resolves itself in simplicity, in unity. It is drawn from his treatise *On Loving God*:

> Happy the man who . . . no longer even loves himself except for God. "O God, your justice is like the mountains of God."[1] This love is a mountain, God's towering peak. Truly indeed, it is the fat, fertile mountain. "Who will climb the mountain of the Lord?"[2] "Who will give me the wings of a dove, that I may fly away to find rest?"[3] . . . When will this sort of affection be felt that, inebriated with divine love, the mind may forget itself and become in its own eyes like

1. Ps 96.
2. Ps 24.
3. Ps 55.

a broken dish,[4] hastening towards God and clinging to him, becoming one with him in spirit,[5] saying "My flesh and my heart have wasted away; O God of my heart, O God, my share for eternity."[6] I would say that man is blessed and holy to whom it is given to experience something of this sort, so rare in life, even if it be but once and for the space of a moment. To lose yourself, as if you no longer existed, to cease completely to experience yourself, to reduce yourself to nothing is not a human sentiment but a divine experience. If any mortal, suddenly rapt, as has been said, and for a moment is admitted to this, immediately the world of sin envies him: . . . "Unhappy man that I am, who will free me from this body doomed to death?"[7]

All the same, since Scripture says God made everything for his own purpose, the day must come when the work will conform to and agree with its Maker. It is therefore necessary for our souls to reach a similar state in which, just as God willed everything to exist for himself, so we wish that neither ourselves nor other beings to have been nor to be except for his will alone; not for our pleasure. The satisfaction of our wants, chance happiness, delights us less than to see his will done in us and for us, which we implore every day in prayer saying: ". . . your will be done on earth as it is in heaven . . ."

As a drop of water seems to disappear completely in a big quantity of wine, even assuming the wine's taste and color; just as red, molten iron becomes so much like fire it seems to lose its primary state; just as the air on a sunny day seems transformed into sunshine instead of being lit up; so it is necessary for the saints that all human feelings melt in a mysterious way and flow into the will of God. Otherwise, how will God be all in all[8] if something human survives in man? No doubt, the substance remains though under another form, another glory, another power. When will this happen? Who will see it? Who will possess it? "When shall

4. Ps 31.
5. 1 Cor 6:17.
6. Ps 73.
7. Rom 7:24.
8. 1 Cor 15:28.

I come and when shall I appear in God's presence?"[9] O my Lord, my God, "My heart said to you: my face has sought you; Lord, I will seek your face."[10] Do you think I shall see your holy temple?[11]

9. Ps 42.
10. Ps 27.
11. Bernard, Dil X.28; CF 13B:29–31.

BIBLIOGRAPHY

Adam of Perseigne, *Epistolæ*; Translated by Grace Perigo, *The Letters of Adam of Perseigne*, Cistercian Fathers Series 21, Kalamazoo: Cistercian Publications, 1976.

Aelred of Rievaulx, *De institutione inclusarum*; Translated by Mary Paul MacPherson, ocso, "A Rule of Life for a Recluse," in *Treatises; The Pastoral Prayer*, Cistercian Fathers Series 2, Kalamazoo: Cistercian Publications, 1971.

———, *De spirituali amicitia*; Translated by Mary Eugenia Laker, ssnd, *Spiritual Friendship*, Cistercian Fathers Series 5, Kalamazoo: Cistercian Publications, 1977.

———, *Speculum caritatis*; Translated by Elizabeth Connor, ocso, *The Mirror of Charity*, Cistercian Fathers Series 17, Kalamazoo: Cistercian Publications, 1990.

———, *The Liturgical Sermons: The First Clairvaux Collection, Sermons One–Twenty-eight, Advent–All Saints*; Translated by Theodore Berkeley, ocso, and M. Basil Pennington, ocso, Cistercian Fathers Series 58, Kalamazoo: Cistercian Publications, 2001.

Baldwin of Ford, *Spiritual Tractates*, Volume One, Tractates I–VIII; Translated by David N. Bell, Cistercian Fathers Series 39, Kalamazoo: Cistercian Publications, 1986.

———, *Spiritual Tractates*, Volume Two, Tractates IX–XVI; Translated by David N. Bell, Cistercian Fathers Series 41, Kalamazoo: Cistercian Publications, 1986.

Bernard of Clairvaux, *Liber de diligendo Deo*; with an analytical commentary by Emero Stiegman, *On Loving God*, Cistercian Fathers Series 13B, Kalamazoo: Cistercian Publications, translation 1973, commentary 1995.

———, *Epistolæ*; Translated by Bruno Scott James, *The Letters of St Bernard of Clairvaux*, Kalamazoo: Cistercian Publications, 1998.

———, *Liber de gradibus humilitatis et superbiae;* Translated by M. Ambrose Conway, ocso, *The Steps of Humility and Pride,* Cistercian Fathers Series 13A, Kalamazoo: Cistercian Publications, 1973.

———, *Sermones super* Cantica canticorum *1–20;* Translated by Kilian Walsh, ocso, *On the Song of Songs I,* Cistercian Fathers Series 4, Kalamazoo: Cistercian Publications, 1971.

———, *Sermones super* Cantica canticorum *21–46;* Translated by Kilian Walsh, ocso, *On the Song of Songs II,* Cistercian Fathers Series 7, Kalamazoo: Cistercian Publications, 1983.

———, *Sermones super* Cantica canticorum *47–66;* Translated by Kilian Walsh, ocso, and Irene Edmonds, *On the Song of Songs III,* Cistercian Fathers Series 31, Kalamazoo: Cistercian Publications, 1979.

———, *Sermones super* Cantica canticorum *67–86;* Translated by Irene Edmonds, *On the Song of Songs IV,* Cistercian Fathers Series 40, Kalamazoo: Cistercian Publications, 1980.

Gilbert of Hoyland, *Sermones super* Cantica canticorum, volume 1; Translated by Lawrence C. Braceland, sj, *Sermons on the Song of Songs, I,* Cistercian Fathers Series 14, Kalamazoo: Cistercian Publications, 1978.

———, *Sermones super* Cantica canticorum, volume 2; Translated by Lawrence C. Braceland, sj, *Sermons on the Song of Songs, II,* Cistercian Fathers Series 20, Kalamazoo: Cistercian Publications, 1979.

———, *Sermones super* Cantica canticorum, volume 3; Translated by Lawrence C. Braceland, sj, *Sermons on the Song of Songs, III,* Cistercian Fathers Series 26, Kalamazoo: Cistercian Publications, 1979.

———, *Treatises, Epistles, and Sermons with Roger of Byland, The Milk of Babes;* Translated by Lawrence C. Braceland, sj, Cistercian Fathers Series 34, Kalamazoo: Cistercian Publications, 1981.

Guerric of Igny, *Liturgical Sermons,* volume 1; Translated by Monks of Mount Saint Bernard Abbey, Cistercian Fathers Series 8, Shannon, Ireland: Irish University Press, 1971.

———, *Liturgical Sermons,* volume 2; Translated by Monks of Mount Saint Bernard Abbey, Cistercian Fathers Series 32, Kalamazoo: Cistercian Publications, 1971.

Isaac of Stella, *Sermons on the Christian Year;* Translated by Hugh McCaffery, Cistercian Fathers Series 11, Kalamazoo: Cistercian Publications, 1979.

John of Ford, *Super extremam partem* Cantici canticorum *sermones cxx,* volume 1; Translated by Wendy Mary Beckett, Cistercian Fathers Series 29, Kalamazoo: Cistercian Publications, 1977.

————, *Super extremam partem* Cantici canticorum *sermones cxx,* volume 7; Translated by Wendy Mary Beckett, Cistercian Fathers Series 47, Kalamazoo: Cistercian Publications, 1984.

Migne, J.-P., *Patrologiæ cursus completus, series latina.* 221 volumes. Paris, 1844–1864.

Walter Daniel, *Vita Aelredi;* Translated by F. M. Powicke, Cistercian Fathers Series 57, Kalamazoo: Cistercian Publications, 1994.

William of St Thierry, *De contemplando Deo, Oratio domni Willelmi, Meditative orationes;* Translated by Sister Penelope, csmv, *On Contemplating God, Prayer, Meditations,* Cistercian Fathers Series 3, Kalamazoo: Cistercian Publications, 1977.

————, *Enigma fidei;* Translated by John D. Anderson, *The Enigma of Faith,* Cistercian Fathers Series 9, Kalamazoo: Cistercian Publications, 1973.

————, *Epistola [aurea] ad fratres de Monte Dei;* Translated by Theodore Berkeley, ocso, *The Golden Epistle: A Letter to the Brethren at Mont Dieu,* Cistercian Fathers Series 12, Kalamazoo: Cistercian Publications, 1980.

————, *Expositio in epistolam Pauli* ad Romanos; Translated by John Baptist Hasbrouck, *Exposition on the* Epistle to the Romans, Cistercian Fathers Series 27, Kalamazoo: Cistercian Publications, 1980.

————, *Expositio super* Cantica canticorum; Translated by Mother Columba Hart, osb, *Exposition on the* Song of Songs, Cistercian Fathers Series 6, Kalamazoo: Cistercian Publications, no date.

————, *De natura et dignitate amoris;* Translated by Thomas X. Davis, *The Nature and Dignity of Love,* Cistercian Fathers Series 30, Kalamazoo: Cistercian Publications.

————, *Speculum fidei;* Translated by Thomas X. Davis, *The Mirror of Faith,* Cistercian Fathers Series 15, Kalamazoo: Cistercian Publications, 1979.

————, *Sancti Bernardi vita prima;* In *Bernard of Clairvaux: Early Biographies. Volume I by William of St. Thierry, Centennial Edition: 1090–1990,* Guadalupe Translations, Lafayette, OR, 1990.

INDEX OF SCRIPTURE CITATIONS

INDEX OF CITATIONS FROM THE CISTERCIAN FATHERS

GENERAL INDEX